Geoffrey Dimbleby is Professor of Human Environment at the Institute of Archaeology, London University. He is primarily a botanist who has turned his attention to the study of plants and plant evidence in archaeology. He lives in St Albans.

Geoffrey Dimbleby

Plants and Archaeology

PALADIN
GRANADA PUBLISHING
London Toronto Sydney New York

Published by Granada Publishing Limited
in Paladin 1978

ISBN 0 586 08282 4

First published by John Baker Publishers Ltd 1967
Copyright © G. W. Dimbleby 1967

Granada Publishing Limited
Frogmore, St Albans, Herts AL2 2NF
and
3 Upper James Street, London W1R 4BP
1221 Avenue of the Americas, New York, NY 10020, USA
117 York Street, Sydney, NSW 2000, Australia
100 Skyway Avenue, Toronto, Ontario, Canada M9W 3A6
Trio City, Coventry Street, Johannesburg 2001, South Africa
CML Centre, Queen & Wyndham, Auckland 1, New Zealand

Made and printed in Great Britain by
Richard Clay (The Chaucer Press) Ltd
Bungay, Suffolk
Set in Monotype Ehrhardt

Preface

In the decade since this book was first published the extraction of botanical material from archaeological sites has greatly increased. In revising the text for the present edition, the significance of this new material has been taken into account, though it is clearly not possible in a short book to give many actual examples. On the whole the basic structure of the book remains unchanged, for the new developments have in effect filled out the various topics which the original layout of the book covered. One chapter, that on 'Cultivated Plants', has been extensively re-written, and the list of references greatly increased.

I acknowledge the help and advice given by colleagues, and in particular the critical reading of the text of the first edition by Professor J. D. Evans and Professor P. J. Newbould, from the archaeological and ecological points of view respectively. I have taken account of criticisms and suggestions made since the original publication, and hope that this new edition will prove an acceptable synthesis of many points of view.

The book has been re-illustrated, though one or two plates and the line drawings are retained. Most of the new photographic work is again by Mr Philip Porter, of the Institute of Archaeology, and it will be agreed that the high quality of the work in the first edition has been surpassed in the new plates. I am glad to acknowledge again the help of Mr John Shaw, lately of the Department of Forestry, Oxford, who drew Figure 4.

Finally, I acknowledge the contributions made by a generation of students who have used this book and commented on it, not least the student who paid me the compliment of appropriating our library copy a short time after it appeared on the shelves!

G. W. DIMBLEBY

Contents

List of Illustrations

Well and badly grown oaks
Pine cones from waterlogged deposit. Thatcham
Box. Winterton
Seeds. Beckford
Seeds. Silbury
Seeds. Cereals – charred
Moss
Transverse section of charcoal of Traveller's Joy (*Clematis*)
Tree rings
Modern pollen and spores
Old pollen and spores
Silica skeletons
Leaf impressions

Line Drawings

Introduction

In principle I am opposed to the writing of this book. Being trained as an ecologist makes me constantly aware that an artificial distinction is being made by dealing only with man's relationships with plants and omitting the animal kingdom, geology, soils and other components of the environment. Whether one considers the wide ecological setting or restricts attention to the use of raw materials and foodstuffs, only half the story is told if only the plant kingdom is dealt with. Why, then, has this basic principle been ignored? The reasons are essentially practical. In fact, we have a parallel in ecology itself. All ecologists would agree that their subject is a unity embracing the animal and plant kingdoms as well as the inorganic environment, yet there are many ecologists who are either plant ecologists or animal ecologists; there are even splinter groups such as tropical plant ecologists or applied ecologists. The subject is in fact so huge that it is very difficult for one person to be equally proficient in all its aspects; moreover, there are basic differences between plants and animals which make it necessary to employ quite different methods of study. To take but one factor: plants are static and animals are mobile, a factor which mattered a great deal to early man. So for purely practical reasons this book will be confined to botany, even though at times it seems illogical to leave out other aspects.

This decision is made the more reasonable because books have already been published on specialized subjects such as soils, geology, and several aspects of zoology in relation to archaeology. Nothing comparable has been published for the plant world, despite the fact that botany has already made considerable contributions to archaeology through many discrete and uncoordinated observations. In the Introduction to the first edition of this book the plea was made to archaeologists to recognize that most sites contain some plant remains, because this material could form the basis of interpretation of landscape and land use, as well as of cultural activities involving plants. The plea is now unnecessary; in the intervening decade plant material has come out of archaeological sites in an embarrassing abundance, and it is now regarded as part of the excavation routine to extract such material. This change has largely been brought about by the development of flotation techniques for the extraction of carbonized seeds, a process which also brings to light other small plant and animal remains.

Whilst such work is primarily done from the immediate standpoint of man's cultural activities, it makes the point that sites can hold unexpected riches of this sort. Interpretation may go far beyond the obvious and immediate significance of the food plants, and comparative studies of different periods or geographical areas can build up a corpus of knowledge about plant geography and ecology.

As one who has come into archaeology from the field sciences, I have long thought that the archaeologist should be aware of the potential scientific value of ancient sites. Indeed, I see no reason why archaeology should have exclusive claim on sites occupied by ancient man; they are equally important for botanists, pedologists and zoologists. This, of course, is how the subject has grown up, and it has not been helped by the fact that the scientific specialists themselves have not been alive to the value of what sites can hold. Nevertheless, the archaeologist is not justified in liquidating a site without reference to other possible interests; even more to be deplored is the attitude that once a site has been excavated archaeologically it is finished with and can be filled in or bulldozed flat. In fact, I think that responsibility for ancient monuments should be shared with whatever organization exists for the conservation of nature. This would emphasize that sites are valuable not only for the history of man, but for the history of his environment, with which he is inextricably bound up.

In recent years there has been a spate of books on archaeology dealing with cultures, technology, regions, ages and so forth, but hardly ever do they reveal any interest in the landscape in which man was living; still less do they reveal any awareness that man was inevitably modifying that landscape. This is why this book sets out to give more than just a catalogue of the uses of plants to man, but includes the environmental component as one of the essential parameters.

One of the problems of 'archaeobotany' is that it is sometimes easier to identify the material than interpret the identifications. For this reason it is necessary to consider man's relationship with plants in the widest sense, so that we have some idea of whether the plants found on sites got there by accident, through natural growth or through man's own deliberate efforts. Often, of course, it is not possible to reach a firm conclusion on such a point, but it is in the hope of showing some of the possibilities that the first part of the book is designed. The second part presents the way plant material is preserved, and the third gives a basis for interpreting man's influence on his surroundings through his use of plants or through his impact on vegetation. As new lines of enquiry open up, new contributions are being made in this field, but underlying all these are the fundamental considerations of how plant material found its way on to a site, how it can be isolated and identified, and how it can be interpreted. It is hoped that this book will provide a useful treatment of these basic themes.

PART

Man's Place in Space

Part 1

Man's use of plants

I

Vegetation – the background to human life

In what way is man most dependent upon the plant world? Today the answer to this would probably vary according to whether the question were asked of a townsman or a countryman, but both would no doubt be thinking of plants primarily as sources of food and raw materials. These necessities, of course, always have been important, but for primitive man there may have been other considerations of equal importance. Even today disasters occur because the vegetation clothing the earth has been damaged or destroyed, and in earlier times, when man lived much closer to the earth, quite small disruptions of the natural balance could have had severe repercussions for whole families, villages or tribes. So before we turn in detail to the multifarious ways in which man used plants, it is well to put human life in perspective against the broader background; that is, to look at man in his natural habitat.

Through the millions of years in which evolution has been taking place, progress in the animal and plant kingdoms has gone hand in hand. If one gets the impression from geology textbooks that animal fossils are much more common than those of plants, this is only a reflection of the fact that plants have less resistant structural members or skeletons and so are less well preserved. Nevertheless plant fossils are found throughout the geological sequence, and we have a fair idea of how the vegetable world has evolved. In this book we are concerned with plants during the time that man has been on the earth. What this time span is depends on how one defines man, but two million years would seem to cover his whole developmental history from the time the genus *Homo* first evolved. Geologically two million years ago is but yesterday, and the plants on the earth were very much the same as they are today; taxonomically, that is, not in distribution. It is difficult to be certain how close the actual species were to those of today, for though two million years is but a tick of the geological clock, it is quite long enough for the fossil plants of that age to have been broken up and the pieces scattered, so that we rarely find the complete plants. Fruits, leaves and stems may all occur separately and though they show us that familiar genera such as pine (*Pinus*) or birch (*Betula*) were present,[78] we cannot say that the species were the same as now.

Nevertheless, it is possible to show that then, as now, the vegetation of the earth's surface was largely determined by climate, and indeed some of the best evidence we have for the climatic fluctuations through the Pleistocene period comes from plant remains.

There are few habitats on the earth's surface where plant life is impossible; even fewer if one includes the microscopic plants. Deserts of extreme aridity, alpine peaks of extreme cold and unstable rocks, regions of permanent ice, and the summits of active volcanoes are such places, but even in these if there is some temporary alleviation of the lethal conditions higher plants may appear, such as the brief glory of the rain flora which springs up in some deserts after a rare fall of rain. The great variety of life form in the higher plants – trees, shrubs, herbs, creepers, climbers, cushion plants, bulb plants and so on – ensure that there are plants to fill the great variety of ecological and climatic habitats which are provided on the surface of the land. Thus we see the tropical rainforest, the temperate deciduous forests, the grasslands of the world, the tundra of the arctic, to mention only a few examples. One of the major effects of this worldwide blanket of vegetation is to soften the impact of the great physical forces which are for ever at work on the land surface: the effects of temperature extremes, frost or tropical heat, in fragmenting a rock surface; the erosive powers of wind and water. Even in temperate climates these forces from time to time become extreme, and at high altitudes, or in the high and low latitudes, they can be severe most of the time. The cover of vegetation has a moderating effect, reducing the extremes of temperature at the ground surface, breaking the force of the rain, and, through the soil which it builds up, reducing the rate of water flow off the land. In other words, the forces of denudation are to some extent tamed where vegetation is able to grow. Forest obviously can exert the greatest control over the soil, though it is surprising how effective even a poor grass cover can be.

This elementary fact was probably one of the most important factors in the daily life of early man. The very forces which are so powerful in the weathering of the land surfaces are also those which, when they are extreme, are distinctly unfavourable to man, especially primitive man. It is not easy for us to appreciate the benefit of the shelter which vegetation – more especially tall vegetation such as forest or scrub – provides. Not only do we live in our own artificial shelters, but the countryside around us has long since lost its forest cover and is suffering from exposure to the elements. There is no better way to appreciate the moderating influence of forest cover than to walk over the moors on a windy winter's day until one comes to a forest plantation. Deep in the plantation the air is still though the tops of the trees may be lashed by the wind; evaporation is reduced so the body feels warmer. Equally on a hot summer's day the same wood will give shade from the sun. Indeed it is likely that the loss of shelter through deforestation could in itself be enough to render some places uninhabitable, at any rate at certain seasons.

Apart from shelter and shade there are other features of the well-vegetated landscape which are of basic importance to man. Before agriculture was introduced man was dependent for his livelihood on what the environment could provide. The importance of animals, especially the larger herbivores, in human economy does not form part of our subject; nevertheless, it is obvious that animal life is directly or indirectly dependent ultimately on the green plant. The various great plant formations of the world, such as the tundra, boreal, temperate or tropical forest, the savannas or the grasslands vary greatly in their ability to carry stock whether wild or domestic (Butzer, 1971), so that man's way of life has frequently been governed by this simple relationship. The large herbivores themselves constituted an important ecological factor, for the stability of the vegetation depended upon their numbers. If they were too numerous they could bring about dramatic changes, sometimes amounting to destruction of the habitat, by eating out the range; if they were too few the character of the vegetation might change, perhaps from grassland to some form of scrub or forest. In order to maintain stability in any plant community there is a balance between all the organisms concerned, plants and animals, which if upset may result in a change of the whole ecosystem. The effect of man in such a system is often crucial, particularly where his interests impinge directly upon the larger grazing animals which are so potent an ecological factor. Early man probably existed in numbers too small to be of great consequence, though even in pre-agricultural times the uncontrolled use of fire in grasslands and savanna areas probably had an effect out of all proportion to the populations involved.[154] In later times, particularly in the historic period, when killing power was greatly increased by the introduction of firearms, the balance has been totally upset. Thus the bison has been eliminated from the North American plains, and the caribou in the Barrens of Canada is decimated in numbers. Where man is dependent upon these animals and is unable to change his way of life, he himself is threatened with extinction. This indeed seems to be the inevitable fate of those Eskimos who are absolutely dependent upon the caribou.[114]

The concept of stability or equilibrium in vegetation is fundamental to ecology. If a new land surface is exposed, as for instance by landslide, by volcanic discharge or by a fall in sea or lake levels, vegetation immediately begins to colonize the new ground. The first stages may be slow and apparently insignificant, but in due course the surface becomes covered with green plants. In this country, coltsfoot (*Tussilago farfara*) is a common invader of unstabilized new ground such as roadsides and railway embankments, but in due course it is followed and superseded by grasses and many associated herbs, together with the occasional shrub such as goat willow (*Salix caprea*) or even pioneer trees like birch or sycamore (*Acer pseudoplatanus*). In perhaps 50–100 years the place will be forested, but even so changes continue. The trees which came in as pioneers are relatively short-lived, 100–200 years, and as they die out they are replaced by more long-lived trees which make greater demands on the habitat than the pioneers did. Thereafter change slows down until, in theory at any rate, the composition of this forest remains constant; that is, equilibrium is reached. Ecologists are by no means agreed about the nature of this equilibrium, or even whether it is ever in fact achieved, but it is generally accepted that a process of succession leads progressively to more highly organized communities of organisms which are converging towards a balanced condition. One reason why it is so difficult to decide on the nature of this supposed equilibrium is that there is practically nowhere on the earth now where man has not interfered with the natural balance, so that we have no field material which can be studied as a control.

Whether or not equilibrium is actually achieved, there is apparently a tendency towards it, and as already mentioned, as the succession proceeds, the community becomes more complex in organization. An example of this increasing complexity might be as illustrated at the top of page 21.

Not only is the complexity becoming greater above the ground, but as the vegetation becomes more diversified so it becomes more complex below the ground. Roots, rhizomes and other underground organs exploit the soil to the full depth to which rooting is possible. In other words, there has been a progressive increase in the exploitation by the vegetation both of the air-space above ground and the potential rooting volume beneath.

Bare ground colonized by algae and lichens

↓

Grasses and herbs (1 layer)

↓

Pioneer shrubs and trees scattered in
grass cover (2 layers)

↓

Pioneer trees, underwood of shrubs and
young trees; ground flora (3 layers)

↓

Forest of mixed ages (several layers) with many
microhabitats, e.g. dead logs and stumps.

When the ultimate equilibrium is reached this can therefore be seen to represent the maximum utilization of the habitat which can be achieved by those plants geographically available to the site. To put this another way, such a community represents the greatest build-up of living organic matter which is possible on that site – again with the species available in the area (Ashby, 1969). Such a highly organized stable community is called a climax.

The nature of the climax depends upon a number of factors, but climate is the most important one. In ecology, however, it is rarely possible to pick out one factor in isolation from all others, and this is certainly true of climax communities. Climate will generally determine whether the dominant vegetation should be coniferous forest, deciduous forest or savanna, for instance, but within each broad group (formation) there may be many variants due to differences in the local geology, topography, hydrology and so on. In extreme cases, as for instance where water is permanently near the surface, even the characteristic vegetation type of the region may be unable to develop. Reedswamp may occur in such places in a region which is climatically suited to forest. In general, however, wherever climate is similar, the type of climax will be similar. Regions in the tropics where the rainfall is heavy all the year round will have tropical rain forest, whether they are in Asia, Africa or South America. The Mediterranean type of climate goes with a flora of evergreen trees with leathery leaves, whether it be in Europe, California or Australia. The species may be totally different in each of these places, yet the overall appearance of the vegetation is much the same. This is of some importance to man when he wants to introduce plants from one region to another. If he can match up climates, then he is much more likely to succeed in introducing the exotics. However, there are many cases where successful introductions have been made in spite of considerable differences in habitat. For instance, the sycamore is quite at home in Britain, regenerating itself vigorously and competing very successfully with the native trees. Yet it has only been introduced into Britain during the historical period, perhaps as recently as the fifteenth century.[91] On the Continent its native distribution is strongly South European, where it occurs in the mountainous areas south of the Alps.

The recognizable relationship between climax vegetation and climate is of fundamental importance in our studies of climatic sequences in the past. From plant remains and particularly from the pollen of past vegetation which is preserved in peat bogs and other media, it is possible to say that one assemblage of remains indicates tundra, whilst another may indicate mixed deciduous forest. Immediately it is obvious that the first represents cold conditions, and the second temperate conditions with well-distributed rainfall. Knowing what we do of the ecological preferences of certain species, sometimes similar deductions can be made from the presence of remains of such critical species (indicators). In general it is safer to base such conclusions on whole assemblages of species (communities) rather than upon individual species. The present distribution of a species may not be a good guide to its real potentialities, as we have seen with sycamore, so that at other times and in other places its habitat preference may have been different. Furthermore, ecological factors have an awkward habit of compensating for each other in a way which is not easy to forecast. Another potential source of error when working with single species derives from the point made earlier that vegetation – and especially forest vegetation – tends to create its own microclimate. A tree such as alder (*Alnus glutinosa*) is seen today as a riverside species, and it is generally assumed therefore that it likes waterlogged habitats. During the Atlantic period (see Chapter 13) it was apparently a component of the forest which clothed Europe, and this has led people to infer that rainfall was so high at this time (and there is no question that it was a relatively wet period) that the soils were permanently waterlogged. But it seems more likely that alder is a tree which requires *adequate* soil water in the spring for the establishment of its seeds.[104] Today it can only find this along streamsides, because as a result of our almost total deforestation this is the only habitat where such moisture conditions are guaranteed. But if the forests were allowed to cover the landscape again even now I think it likely that alder would once more become a general component of the forest. Under a widespread forest cover there would be equable moisture conditions all the year round, which is not the case in small blocks of forest or open country such as make up our present landscape. The use of individual indicator species therefore, can be risky, whereas a whole assemblage of plants is much less likely to be a source of error. This is not to decry the very great contribution which such studies have made to our knowledge of past climates; in many cases there can be no question of what the presence of a certain species implies. Such a case would be mountain avens (*Dryas octopetala*), a plant of dwarf habit and with a tolerance of cold conditions which would only survive in cold arctic, alpine or other habitats where the growth of taller plants was impossible. Its occurrence in certain periods of the Late-glacial, therefore, is a safe basis for climatic interpretation (Godwin, 1975). Nevertheless, it is unfortunately true that the requirements of many plants used in this way are not so well authenticated. Too often their ecological preferences are deduced from their present distributions, and too seldom is there solid physiological evidence to support this.

However, our interpretation of past climatic conditions does not rest solely upon the evidence of vegetable remains. Geomorphology, soils, river and stream systems, and animal remains are some of the complementing lines of approach which can provide a good check on the conclusions obtained from the botanical data (Butzer, 1971). The changes of climate and flora which have taken place through the Pleistocene and Postglacial periods are not properly the subject of this book; but here we should make note not so much of the enormously interesting and important facts of climatic change and their significance in dating, but of the more ecological aspect, since each vegetation type represents a different habitat, a different set of conditions which favour man's existence or which militate against it. It was against this varied ecological background that he had to work out his way of life: gathering and hunting, especially of the larger game animals; or perhaps herding; or, in appropriate places, agriculture. The use which he was able to make of the land in turn determined what sort of impact he made upon the landscape. Clearly hunting will have had much less effect on the vegetation (unless fire was used where the fire hazard was high) than will agriculture. Referring back to what was said earlier about climax vegetation being the maximum utilization of the potentialities of the habitat, it follows that any man-made or man-induced community will represent a lower level of utilization. It may mean even more. It may mean that the ecological equilibrium had been destroyed, so that the protective effect of vegetation against the physical weathering processes became so reduced that they were able to prevail and seriously degrade or even destroy the biological habitat. Against this perpetual working of the physical forces of the habitat must be set the restorative powers of the biological world, working through succession towards a new climax. Though man may use the land for gain, in doing so he brings about some decrease in fertility, but this can be made good if he will after a time leave the land to restore itself by successional development. Studies of prehistoric agriculture and of present-day land use in primitive societies show that this was learnt early, for there is good evidence of shifting culti-vation in temperate regions in prehistoric times; in the tropics, of course, it is still practised.[12] The land is used until fertility falls off; then it is abandoned to natural regrowth and it may be many years before the same piece of ground is returned to. Under the conditions in which it was devised this system worked well, but as populations have increased the demand on the land has led to shorter and shorter periods of fallow so that the fertility has not been given a chance to build up again. Even in prehistoric times it is likely that something was known about the restoration of fertility by other means such as additions of wood ash or household refuse, and today the use of fertilizers of one sort and another has largely replaced the older practices of fallow and rotation of crops, though these modern methods are not without their problems.

This survey of the place of vegetation as a background to human existence will have demonstrated the complexity of the relationship. It is important to have this background in mind when we are considering the narrower aspects of man's use of plants, and it will be necessary to hark back to these interactions from time to time. Above all it must be realized that the biological world is a complex, interwoven system and that by removing plants or introducing them into the system man is inevitably causing changes which can have unforeseeable consequences. The third part of this book will be dealing particularly with some examples of the changes – good and bad – which man has caused and these will show the far-reaching consequences of his transition from a mere cog in the ecolo-gical wheel to the stage where he dominates and tries to control his environment – an aim in which even now he cannot unequivocally be said to have succeeded.

Wild plants as sources of food and drink

In our modern civilized society our dependence upon wild plants for sustenance is minimal, practically all our vegetable diet coming from plants cultivated in one part of the world or another. At appropriate seasons of the year we may collect blackberries and mushrooms (though even these are coming more and more under commercial control in Britain, quite apart from the cultivated mushroom industry). In regions where such plants are abundant certain seaweeds, edible fungi and berries such as bilberry, wild strawberry and cranberry may be important but generally these are little more than *bonnes bouches* in their season. There are the few individuals, often regarded as cranks, who will make their own concoctions from elderberries, dandelions, crab apples and so forth, but these do not form the staple diet of such enthusiasts. Indeed, if one studies a book on wild foods (e.g.[102]), one is always struck by the fact that these are mostly salads, flavourings and other additives useful in alleviating the monotony of our civilized diet; they are singularly lacking in bulk and solidity. Wild nuts and tubers are generally small and large numbers are needed to make a substantial meal. In fact, if the average modern man were deprived of all cultivated vegetables (including cereals and fruits) and forced to obtain his own wild foods, he would be in a sorry position. Moreover his abysmal ignorance of field botany would give him food for thought on the shortcomings of modern education whilst he waited for the next crop of blackberries to ripen.

Since cultivation has brought about such a complete change in our relationship with wild nature, it follows that it is primarily in the pre-agricultural periods that wild plants were important as the mainstays of life. There are few people in the world today living completely in pre-agricultural conditions, and those who do so are partly dependent upon animal foods. Consequently we have little direct evidence of man's use of the plant kingdom in pre-agricultural times, especially in those parts of the world where cultivation has long been established. In Europe, for instance, our knowledge of what plants mesolithic man used is extremely small and inevitably incomplete, and is entirely dependent on such few botanical remains as are found on archaeological sites. In North America, however, there is not such a complete hiatus between the distant past and the present, for it is partly bridged by the North American Indian. In North America, of course, cultivation was being practised some 1,500 years before the European introduced his methods of agriculture, the cultivation of maize having spread up from Central America where it began thousands of years earlier.[86] Nevertheless, the tradition of food-gathering and using the wild vegetation for other uses had continued alongside the development of agriculture in a way that it had not done in Europe, and when the Europeans first settled in North America they were able to make valuable observations on this aspect of the life of the Indians they encountered. To some extent the tribal system of the Indians favoured this preservation of the old traditions because the tribes varied in their ways of life, some being highly geared to the agricultural economy, others much less so and retaining nomadic traits with which food gathering was associated. Since the European settlement the Indian cultures have largely been subordinated to the European-type economy and much has been lost, yet enough remains from the records of the early settlers and from recent studies on the remnants of Indian cultures to provide us with a fairly comprehensive body of information.

One fundamental point which emerges from such studies is that the way of life of the Indian is closely related to plant ecology, particularly as regards his use of the wild plants for food. This is particularly noticeable in the Lake States region, which lies on the climatic boundary – a broad zone, not a hard line – between the boreal (coniferous) forests to the north and the mixed deciduous forests farther south. The poorer soils and the less favourable climate of the coniferous forests result in a relatively poor flora containing few plants of use to man. This forced men living in the north to depend to a much greater degree on animal rather than plant foods; agriculture, for the same reasons, was practically excluded from the northern part of this territory. Ecologists have shown that in any biologically balanced community there is a relationship between the vegetation, the herbivorous animals and the carnivores which is usually described as the pyramid of numbers (Fig. 1). On this basis, it will be seen that if a man moves from being largely a plant-eater (herbivore) to an animal-eater (carnivore), the population which a unit area of ground is able to sustain is going to diminish as he moves farther up the order of predation towards the apex of the pyramid. This is in fact what we find: that cultures dependent on animal food are considerably less numerous per unit area than those which depend more on plant foods. In other words, the population density is less.

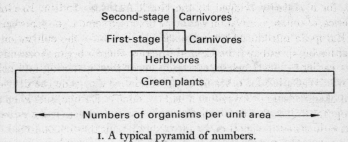

1. A typical pyramid of numbers.

By drawing upon what we know of the uses of plants made by modern Indians, together with the botanical evidence which has come from archaeological excavations, it is possible to make a rough estimate of the proportion of the flora which was used by the Indians in North America. Restricting our attention to the higher plants – flowering plants, conifers and ferns – it has been calculated that of the 2,000 or so plants native in the Upper Great Lakes region some 4–500 have been used by man, more than a third of them for food (Yarnell, 1964). In view of the fact that many of these plants provide several products, this represents a very considerable exploitation of the available wild plant resources.

The nutritive properties of plant foods depend, of course, upon the quantity of carbohydrates, proteins, and oils in the materials eaten; that is, upon the foods concentrated in plant tissues. Man in fact eats what the plant had provided for its own use. Consequently we may consider the various types of plant organ which we use for food from this standpoint. Where there is seasonality in the climate, the plant will tend to store up food to tide it over the unfavourable season, and once growth is possible again it will mobilize and translocate these reserves to the growing tissues. Man is therefore likely to help himself with greatest effect by using storage tissue or growing tissue, or by intercepting the food as it passes from one to the other.

By following this sequence through the seasons in temperate latitudes it is possible to build up, at least in outline, a picture of the diet of food-gathering people through the course of a year. In what follows the plants mentioned are those known to have been used as food in Europe or Eastern North America; there are close similarities in the floras of the two regions at the level of genus, though species are usually different. The North American flora, however, has a greater number of tree species, many of which are important as food; as we shall see, this may be of some advantage. A great deal of what follows is based on the observations collected by Yarnell (1964).

Early in the spring the foods available to man are very limited. There are no actively growing parts of the plant, and such green foliage as survives the winter is tough and low in food value. Over-wintering food storage organs, however, exist if they can be located. Plants of the lily family (Liliaceae) were used in this way; the bulbs of the wild onion (*Allium*) and the rhizomes of Solomon's Seal (*Polygonatum*), the latter lying near the surface so that they are easily found. A nutritious and tasty sort of 'oatcake' can be made from the rhizomes of bracken (*Pteridium aquilinum*) (Johnson, 1867). The storage organs of water plants were also favoured, perhaps because they also could be obtained relatively easily by being fished up from the mud at the bottom of ponds and lakes. The tubers of the yellow water-lily (*Nuphar*), arrowhead (*Sagittaria*) and bulrush (*Schoenoplectus*) are examples. Here we have a close parallel with the use made of three species of lotus (*Nymphaea*) in Ancient Egypt.[128] The rhizomes of all three were prized as a source of flour. Helbaek found tubers of *Scirpus* at Çatal Hüyük and was puzzled as to their purpose.[74] It seems likely that they were being used as food in this part of Turkey in the 6th millennium B.C.

At this time of the year the trees are waking up from their winter dormancy; as soon as the frost is out of the ground in the rooting zone the roots start to take up water and then the sap starts to flow up the trunks. This sap is rich in sugars which have been mobilized from the stored starch and so constitutes a valuable food source. The best-known example of this type of food is maple syrup, prepared from the sap of the sugar maple, but other species of tree also produce abundant sap, notably the birches, lime, aspen and other species of maple, any of which would doubtless have been an acceptable food source.

As spring advances other foods become available in addition to the continuing supply of underground storage organs and tree sap. The first new greenery begins to appear and it is probable that many types of foliage were eaten at this stage, before it became less succulent and more fibrous as the year progressed. There is direct evidence that the North

American Indians used fern fronds, for example of fiddle fern or bracken, when they were still in the unexpanded stage; bracken can be the cause of fatal physiological disorders in cattle, horses, pigs and rodents[52] and it would be interesting to establish whether the lethal agents are present in the young fronds. The young staminate cones of pine and buds of trees such as lime, which would be a rich source of protein, were apparently also used for food.

In the spring a new and important source of food becomes available, more particularly in the deciduous forest rather than the coniferous forest region. This is the cambium and associated tissues immediately beneath the bark of trees. At this time of the year the trees are beginning to start their growth, and this affects not only the twigs, leaves and flower-buds but also the trunk. In the spring the main diameter growth of the trunk begins, brought about by a single layer of cells – the cambium – which ensheaths the trunk, laying down new tissue which will develop into phloem on the outside and xylem or wood on the inside (Fig. 3). During this active period when tree tissues are differentiating, there is a considerable thickness of young cells rich in proteins and carbohydrates, and this formed an important staple food. Even in modern society this food is still used – the so-called slippery elm – and is a highly nutritious and digestible diet for invalids with gastric disorders. One particular species of elm (*Ulmus rubra*) is its source, but a number of other trees have been used in this way by the North American Indians, and it is reasonable to assume that closely related species would have been used in the same way in Europe. These include, in addition to elms, poplar (or aspen), ash, lime and even pine. This no doubt constituted one of the 'bulk' foods which, on first sight, appear to be so lacking in pre-agricultural times. Indeed a form of bread, the so-called bark bread, has been made from these tissues in Scandinavia until comparatively recent times, the species used being primarily elm (*Ulmus glabra*), though in times of famine even Scots pine (*Pinus sylvestris*) has been used.[116] Pine bark bread, however, far from being a palliative for digestive troubles, is liable to cause them if it is used exclusively. It might be mentioned in passing that the widespread use of such a food-source would inevitably have had an effect on the composition of the forest, for the removal of the living tissues would at least reduce the vigour and reproduction of the species favoured, and at worst, by ringing them, would kill them.

As the spring gives way to early summer the choice of foods becomes much greater, particularly in greens and salads. Reference to any book on wild foods will show that even today a large number of plants in our flora can be and is used in this way, and research into Indian practices in North America reveals many more that are neglected today. To our modern palate many of these will appear tasteless and perhaps texturally unacceptable. We are used to the succulent flesh of cultivated vegetables and to us a vegetable which is tough, fibrous and stringy is unpleasant. Even early man no doubt appreciated good cooking which could reduce the toughest vegetable – such as young twigs of lime trees – to a manageable condition, but there is good evidence that grinding and pounding of food were a regular practice. Some vegetables are too mucilaginous for our Western tastes, though they may be appreciated in other parts of the world. This would apply to young fern shoots, which have already been mentioned, and to the leaves of mallows (*Malva*) which otherwise are perfectly edible.[76] The standards by which the overfed members of Western civilization judge the acceptability of food are probably very different from those of people to whom the collecting of an adequate food-supply is the first necessity of life. It should be remembered, however, when we are considering palatability, that the wild flora contains a much wider variety of plants that can be used for flavouring than ever appeared in a herb garden, so that an enforced staple diet of dull taste could be rendered more interesting in a variety of ways.

Certain families of plants have been particularly useful to man. One of these is the Polygonaceae (Johnson, 1867). Many species in it have astringent and even blistering properties, yet among them are valuable food plants. The root of bistort (*Polygonum bistorta*), for instance, can provide a form of flour once the tannin has been steeped out, and its young shoots can be eaten as greens. Sorrel (*Rumex acetosa*) has long been used as a pleasantly-flavoured salad-plant and for other culinary purposes. However, its leaves contain oxalate and it can be poisonous if eaten in large quantities. It should not be confused with wood sorrel, an unrelated plant having delicate pinky-white flowers and shamrock leaves which have a similar taste and can also be used as a salad or as garnishing. Rhubarb (*Rheum petiolatum*) also contains oxalate in the leaves but the stems (petioles) can be eaten with impunity. Buckwheat (*Fagopyrum esculentum*) has a highly nutritious seed which is eagerly eaten by animals and poultry and has been grown for human consumption since prehistoric times. If eaten in great excess, however, it can produce acute sensitivity to light in animals and in human beings has been suspected of causing brain injury (Johnson, 1867). Its green shoots make good fodder. Seeds of several other species have been found in the Swiss lake-dwellings (Tschumi, 1949). A number of plants in this family have been used as sources of dyes of various colours. Sorrel roots give a red dye and that pernicious weed knotgrass (*Polygonum aviculare*) gives an indigo one (Johnson, 1867).

Another family which provides a variety of diet during the summer is the Umbelliferae. This includes such plants as samphire, fennel (both coastal species) and parsley, but also the wild ancestors of some of our cultivated roots; wild carrot (*Daucus carota*) and wild parsnip (*Pastinaca sativa*) are frequent plants on chalk downs in Britain but their roots are quite insignificant compared with the cultivated forms. Another member of this family produces a small edible tuber which is available from June onwards in Europe; this is the Earth-nut or Pig-nut (*Conopodium majus*). It never seems to have been cultivated but has long been known as a delicious wild food. The huge cow parsnip (*Heracleum maximum*) has been used in North America both as a source of greens and as a root vegetable, and even that garden pest, ground elder (*Aegopodium podagraria*), makes a good green vegetable when the leaves are young.[76] This versatile family includes a number of plants important for their aromatic seeds, such as caraway (*Carum carvi*), but it also includes some highly poisonous members, e.g. the hemlock (*Conium maculatum*). In view of the taxonomic difficulties for the amateur in identifying plants of this family, culinary experimentation should only be made under expert guidance.

The common goosefoot or fat hen (*Chenopodium album*) is a frequent weed of cultivated land and is even thought to have been grown for its own sake in the Bronze Age. It provides a useful source of greens, and its seeds were certainly eaten by prehistoric man. Even in the historic period there are records of its seed having been mixed with wheat to produce a bread meal – a somewhat laxative one, apparently (Johnson, 1867). This plant also occurs as a weed in North America, where it was believed to have been a European introduction, but recently seed caches of this species have been found on archaeological sites which apparently pre-date European influence. Other members of the Chenopodiaceae have also been valuable sources of greenstuff, though now completely neglected.

Not many people would think of eating the leaves of the marsh marigold (*Caltha palustris*), but this species has been so used in North America, and as it occurs widely in Europe it is reasonable to assume that the same applied here also. Another familiar plant which has been, and still is, used as a green vegetable is the stinging nettle (*Urtica dioica*) – also used as a fibre plant. One could go on listing plants which we know once to have been used, or which are still used, as sources of greenstuff; but we must leave it there, merely remarking that this category of food was available throughout the summer and well into the autumn.

By midsummer, however, other categories of food are becoming available. Reference has already been made to the use of the staminate cones of pine as a protein-rich food, and it is perhaps to be expected that many flower buds would have been used in this way. Many flowers provide nectar, as well as being rich in other nutrients. Remains of flowers are seldom preserved but there is evidence of the use of water-lily (*Nymphaea*) flower buds in this way. It seems likely that only large flowers or inflorescences would be worth exploiting, and the water-lily, being supported by water, is one of the most substantial flowers in temperate regions.

Some plants are already well through their annual cycle by mid-summer and the first fruits are beginning to appear. These, naturally, are of those plants which flower early in the year, and those which produce fruits which are edible would have been seized upon by early man as forerunners of the wild harvest to come. There is evidence that mesolithic man in Europe used the seeds of dandelion (*Taraxacum officinale*), vetches (*Vicia* spp.), and of the yellow water-lily (*Nuphar lutea*).[30] Berries and other soft fruits are, of course, adapted to be eaten, and whether the agent be birds or man matters not a bit – the purpose of seed dispersal is achieved. In this sense, man fits much more into the natural ecological pattern when he is feeding on such fruits than when he is destroying the plants upon which he is feeding and contributing no compensatory benefit. Among the early berries to ripen in temperate regions most have been found associated with food-collecting man. For instance, the genus *Ribes* in Britain includes only two species of currant and one gooseberry, but in North America over half a dozen species are known to have been widely used by the Indians. *Vaccinium* shows very much the same pattern; several different species of blueberry were used by the Indians, and in Europe species of both *Ribes* and *Vaccinium* were eaten in mesolithic times.[30] The family Rosaceae contains a great many species whose fruits are adapted to be eaten, among which one must mention, as being useful to man, the following genera: *Prunus* (plums and cherries); *Rubus* (blackberry, raspberry); *Fragaria* (strawberry); *Crataegus* (hawthorn, thornapple – in American parlance); *Pyrus* (pear); *Malus* (apple); *Sorbus* (rowan); *Rosa* (rose); *Mespilus* (medlar); *Amelanchier* (juneberry, North American). Between them these comprise a considerable number of species, some of them common plants, whose fruits ripen from late summer onwards and are often produced in abundance. Seeds, pips, and even complete charred fruits of many species from these genera have been recovered from prehistoric sites both in Europe and in North America.

The development of seed agriculture seems to have been linked very closely with the domestication of members of the grass family: the wheats and barleys, and later rye and oats in the Old World; corn or maize in the New. In the tropics rice, millets and sorghums have all become staple foods, and sugar-cane, though not cultivated for its seed, is another member of the Gramineae. It is therefore surprising to find so little trace of this family's having been of importance to the food-gathering people of temperate latitudes. Some North American Indians ate 'wild rice' (*Zizania aquatica*), but strangely there is only one doubtful record of it in archaeo- logical sites. Its fruit is in no way delicate; in fact, it can withstand burning without serious damage. *Glyceria fluitans*, a floating grass of similar habitat to *Zizania*, has been used as food in Eastern Europe, where it was valued both for its food value and for its flavour.[76] In Western Europe it fruits less abundantly, so may have been less useful there. Helbaek[70] has listed a number of grasses identified from archaeological sites and bog corpses in Denmark, but he gives no suggestion that these were any more than incidental weeds.

As the year approaches its end many plants are providing for the next generation and its dispersal. There are many ways in which this is done, but man is chiefly concerned with those plants which build up a big reserve of food in the seed, in order to provide the newly germinated seedling with a good start when it begins life on its own. This will often be the next spring, though not necessarily; many seeds have a period of enforced dormancy before germination and others are forced by circum- stances to lie dormant, for instance on the forest floor, until conditions are suitable for germination. Sometimes this may entail a rest of tens of years, during which the seed is subject to destruction by animal and fungal predators, and by man. By far the most important group of plants in this category are the trees, many of which produce large seeds with food reserves in the cotyledons or in the endosperm. Few of the conifers come into this category: the stone pine (*Pinus pinea*) produces nuts which were much sought after even in Roman times,[23] and the piñon pine (*P. edulis*) served the Indians of the Great Basin in the same way (Driver, 1964). But neither of these trees is a tree of the northern coniferous forest belt, which once again has little to offer the gatherer of plant food. However, in the deciduous temperate forests there are many examples, a good proportion of which are familiar to us today. The hazel (*Corylus avellana*) nut was undoubtedly a major item in the diet of mesolithic man in Europe, for charred fragments of the shells are found in the occupation layers, the nuts having been cracked open before charring;[132] it is no easy matter to smash them after charring because they become as hard as bullets. In North America at least two species of *Corylus* are known to have been used by the Indians, and a third has been identified from archaeological sites. To mention a point which will be discussed in more detail in a later chapter (Chapter 11), it is significant that though hazel is a component of the mixed deciduous forest it only flowers freely – and therefore only produces nuts abundantly – in full light; this fact was doubtless well known to food-gathering man, and it may be expected that he took steps to favour its reproduction by making clearings. Once again the European tree flora suffers by comparison with that of Eastern North America. The walnut (*Juglans regia*) and the sweet chestnut (*Castanea sativa*) are both trees of the Mediterranean region and are not native in Northern and Western Europe, so they could not have been used by pre-agricultural man in that region. They have both been introduced since, perhaps by the Romans (Godwin, 1975); and it is interesting to note that I have found occasional pollen grains of walnut in the soil buried beneath Iron Age camps in England, suggesting that it, too, was in this country before historic times. In addition to their own species of chestnut (*Castanea dentata*) – now almost eliminated by the chestnut blight introduced from Europe – the North American forests have a number of other edible nuts. The Indians are known to have used butternut (another species of *Juglans*, *J. cinerea*), and several species of *Carya* (hickories), but perhaps most interesting is the observation that beechnuts (*Fagus grandifolia*) and acorns were used on a considerable scale. Moreover, beechnuts and acorns are known from archaeological sites, showing that they have for long been a staple article of diet. This is of direct significance for Europe, for Europe, too, has a beech (*F. sylvatica*) and several species of oak. There seems to be little evidence from archaeological sites of the utilization of these species, but it must remain a strong possibility, particularly as these would provide a bulk food of a type so lacking in the seasonal menu we have been looking at. Beechnuts are, of course, a well-known delicacy today, but to what extent they could have been important to pre-agricultural man in North-west Europe is doubtful. Beech only migrated into North-west Europe late in the Post-glacial, in fact moving hand-in-hand with the spread of agriculture (Godwin, 1975). Pre-agricultural man in Britain and along the western seaboard would therefore have been unfamiliar with beech. Oak is a very different story; this was the dominant tree of the forests of at any rate the later Mesolithic, and though we today regard a diet of acorns with some distaste, the American evidence shows that it would be wrong to attribute our likes to the food-gathering people. Helbaek[74] found acorns in houses of the 6th millennium B.C. at Çatal Hüyük, and points out that boiling or roasting destroys their bitterness. Certainly acorns were widely eaten in North America; out of 60 species 27 are known to have been used. It is true that they needed preparation; various techniques were used for extracting the tannins which they contain, usually involving some form of leaching of the pulped acorns. In California and probably elsewhere, the acorn was the staple food though it was augmented, and in times of acorn shortage, even replaced, by the nuts of the Californian buckeye (*Aesculus californica*), a relative of the horse chestnut. However, not only was this seed considered inferior, but pre-treatment was even more necessary as it contains cyanide (Driver, 1964).

Though on the face of it it appears that the deciduous forest trees had much to offer in the way of food, there is one drawback which was doubtless well known to those who depended on them; that is, that most of these trees do not produce nuts or fruit regularly every year. The reasons for this are partly physiological and probably partly climatic. When a tree produces a very heavy crop of nuts it is obvious that it makes a very heavy demand on its resources in doing so, with the result that over the following years it must build up a new reserve before a new mast can be produced. Different species differ in the interval between masts; in North America the chestnut produces nuts most years, beech, walnut, hickory and some of the oaks every two or three years. The swamp hickory (*Carya cordiformis*), however, may go five years without a good crop, and the white oak (*Q. alba*) ranges from four to ten years. It is remarkable that almost all the trees of any one species behave together in the same pattern; one does not find one individual producing a food crop and another resting. From man's point of view, therefore, there is a distinct advantage to be gained from a forest containing a mixture of species. A bad acorn year, for instance, may be offset by a good crop of beechnuts, and so forth. In Europe there are fewer species in the deciduous forests, and the interval between mast years also varies with species. For beech, for instance, a period of about five years seems to separate really heavy masts, though minor crops do occur in between.[109] On the other hand, mast years for the European oaks are more frequent and predictable.

With the passing of the autumn harvest, the problem of surviving the unproductive winter faced the food gatherers. When the ground was not frozen hard, no doubt underground tubers, bulbs and rhizomes would be used just as they were in early spring. Doubtless, too, attempts were made to store food against the shortages of winter. There is archaeological evidence in the Great Lakes region of the storage of goosefoot seeds, and the Indians are known to have dried currants and wild strawberries, presumably in order to preserve them. It has been shown that the methods used did little harm to the vitamin content (Driver, 1964). Even maple syrup could be preserved for a whole year in vessels made of birch bark, an interesting application of the preservative properties of this bark. But man is not above taking advantage of the provisions that the wild animals have laid up for their own use. Stores of nuts, especially beechnuts, laid down by chipmunks, were a regular source of winter food to certain Indian tribes. The caches made by deermice have also served the same purpose, and apparently arrowhead tubers were taken from muskrat and beaver caches and dried for the winter. Perhaps the greatest single source of food through the winter, however, was the crop of acorns and nuts which had fallen from the trees and become covered over with fallen leaves. Heavy snowfall may restrict this source in some regions, but even after it has gone this food source will still remain. I myself remember making quite a profitable collection of chestnuts from beneath the litter layer in Corsica in April – a bit musty to the taste, perhaps, but still edible.

Looking back over this calendar of menus, we can see that food was available at most times of the year, and that subsistence quantities could have been obtained by people prepared to range far enough afield. The protein value of such a diet, however, was probably inadequate and would need augmenting with meat or fish. But man did not necessarily have to take things as he found them, even in the pre-agricultural era. He had the power to modify his environment, and it would soon have been apparent to him that in doing so he could favour some of the wild species which were important to him as items of food. We have already mentioned the effect that opening up of the forest would have had upon the fruitfulness of the hazel, and the same principle applies to many other species. Furthermore, many of the food plants we have mentioned are not tolerant of deep shade – they only flourish when given sufficient light. This particularly applies to many of the berry-bearing plants, and it is well known that the Indian used fire to reduce the forest and so favour this food source. Moreover, this is effective even in the coniferous forest, and in view of what has been said of the poor supply of vegetable foods that that forest offers, the incentive to clear in this way would be even more marked than in the more productive deciduous forests.

This method of producing more food is indirect. There is evidence that more direct methods were also used, still falling short of genuine food-production by cultivation. There are many examples of plants being found outside their normal range and one explanation would be, at any rate where the plants concerned are of use to man, that he had actually carried them deliberately in the course of his migrations. An example is the pond nut or American lotus (*Nelumbo lutea*) in the Great Lakes area, which has certain northern stations well beyond its general range, and there is every likelihood that it was carried to these places by the Indians. In the same area wild rice is known to have been introduced deliberately into swamps (Driver, 1964). A similar explanation might account for the fact that despite the sporadic appearance of beech in Britain as far back as the Atlantic period, it did not spread *en masse* until the Sub-atlantic. In two cases such occurrence of beech out of context is associated with archaeological occupation; with mesolithic/neolithic remains at High Rocks, Sussex, dated by C^{14} to about 3700 B.C.,[111] and with neolithic remains at Ehenside Tarn in the Lake District, dated to about 3000 B.C.[125] This latter occurrence, however, is now questioned on the grounds of misidentification of the plant remains.

Nevertheless, it is difficult to produce incontrovertible proof of the associations between wild species and man. Plant distribution is so complex in its causes and so little is known about the habitat requirements of individual species, that the geographical result is frequently mystifying. Even less is it possible to detect the hand of man in spreading wild species within their natural range. It would be simple to transfer a useful plant from a somewhat remote spot to a place nearer to one's habitation, and there is evidence that this is being done today. Many of the plants grown in tropical gardens by the native people are apparently uncultivated plants brought in from the wild. As we shall see later, true cultivation nearly always results in detectable genetic differences as compared with the wild parent.

Our discussion has dealt almost entirely with the flowering plants as sources of food, but certain plants of the lower orders have played, and still do so, an important part in the diet of some people. The fungi are an obvious case,[131] and though most of us today limit our exploration of this group to a few easily recognizable species, there can be no doubt that the food-gatherer would be familiar with a much wider variety. Most fungi are strongly seasonal in their appearance, especially in temperate regions, flourishing in autumn when the atmosphere is humid. There are, however, certain perennial fungi which are good to eat, notably the underground truffle (*Tuber* spp.) and the beef-steak fungus (*Fistulina hepatica*), a massive bracket fungus growing on trees. Of more permanent nature than most fungi are the lichens, themselves a symbiotic union of fungus and alga. Again, records of the North American Indian's way of life show that some tribes regularly eat certain lichens which may be found growing on tree-trunks, rocks or even the ground. One of these species is *Cladonia rangiferina*, the reindeer moss which forms the staple food of reindeer and caribou. Though lichens are most abundant in humid climates, many are able to withstand desiccation and so can inhabit places where periodical drought can be prolonged. Rock faces are an obvious example and lichens can even be found in semi-desert areas. The manna which fed the Israelites in the wilderness is thought to be a lichen, *Lecanora esculenta*; certainly such a lichen does grow in the barren tracts of Northern Africa and Western Asia, but there are difficulties in explaining away this miraculous event in this way. One is that to feed an estimated 2 to $2\frac{1}{2}$ million people for forty years would require a prodigious production of lichen – figures range from 2,000 to 9,000 tons per day (Moldenke and Moldenke, 1952).

Apart from the fungi and related lichens the only other non-flowering plants which feature widely as articles of diet are the seaweeds. Being of global occurrence they are even today important foods to many coastal dwellers, and in earlier times they would have been of even greater importance. In Britain today laverbread is eaten in certain parts of the country, made from species of the red seaweed *Porphyra*, or the green *Ulva*. Farrar[50] has shown that the Aztecs of Tenochtitlán (now Mexico City) ate large quantities of a bluish water bloom – apparently a blue-green alga (Cyanophyta) which at certain seasons covered the brackish lake surrounding the city. This was dried into cakes which had a salty, cheesy flavour and also had good keeping qualities.

Archaeological sites seldom reveal much direct evidence of the use of these lower plants because they are mostly fleshy, non-skeletal plants which do not preserve well, but in exceptional conditions of preservation they have been found.[169] The spores of fungi and lichens, however, may be much more resistant to decay, but identification offers serious problems, and interpretation of the occurrence of spores is highly speculative.

It is difficult to divine from the mere occurrence of a plant in an archaeo-logical context just what that plant was used for. Even with those which are solid foods it is not obvious in what form they were eaten – whether raw, cooked, in gruel, porridge or soup, etc. In addition to plants of solid food value, however, there are those which were used primarily for drinks and beverages. Here our interpretation is almost entirely dependent upon what we know of the habits of living peoples. From these it is apparent that many plants were used for the making of beverages; plants widely different in their properties. Moreover, almost any part of the plant has been used. Leaves, fruits, seeds, flowers, bark and roots – all have pro-vided the basis of native drinks in many parts of the world. Drinking is important in the balanced diet, especially for people whose main food is animal flesh. Not only is a large intake of fluid necessary with a high protein diet, but through beverages prepared from plants the essential trace elements and vitamins (especially when the meat is cooked) may be obtained, especially in the winter. It is on record that a concoction, made from the leaves of a tree, probably hemlock (*Tsuga*), has cured scurvy (Yarnell, 1964) – a use for this mighty forest giant which perhaps would not be immediately obvious. Many of the plants concerned are aromatic or have a characteristic flavour, which is no doubt the prime reason for their selection.

In arid areas plants can be a direct source of water or liquid. Some cacti, for instance, store water in their stems in liquid form, and this can readily be extracted. In a similar way the living *Agave* is made to produce agave wine or pulque, rich not only in carbohydrates but also in vitamins B^1 and C. As one plant, before it dies of exhaustion, can produce up to seven quarts of sap a day for as long as six months, it represents an important source of safe drinking liquid in an area where such a commodity is scarce (Driver, 1964). In a different way the vine, too, is a source of liquid, available even at full summer when drought is extreme. A deep-rooting plant, it is able to tap deep resources of water and store it in the fruit. The juice when fermented keeps well and again is a safe source of liquid where water supplies were often suspect. There is not room here to deal at length with fermented liquors, nor is it appropriate in this chapter since the best examples come from cultivated plants, but it may well be that the keeping properties of fermented liquors were equally as important as their role as social lubricants. Linked with the liquid balance of the body is the salt content. Losses can easily be made good within reach of the sea or where there are saline deposits, but elsewhere other sources must be found. Plant ash is one of these, and in parts of Africa today various plants, especially grasses, are burned for this purpose (e.g. [140]).

In this chapter we have been talking mostly about food-gathering in temperate regions – by no means the ideal for human subsistence. As yet little archaeological (though a good deal of anthropological) evidence has come from other climatic regions. Each no doubt presented its problems. The wet tropics with no seasonal differences were probably best able to provide a year-round vegetarian diet (animal food is scarce in many tropical forests), but a dry season in the tropics poses problems of survival parallel with those of the winters of higher latitudes. In all such cases it is apparent that a good deal of the hazard would be taken out of life if man produced his own food, and though this may not be the basic reason for the invention of agriculture, once invented and introduced it would confer distinct advantages, if not the complete sufficiency which we tend to imagine.

Finally, one wonders whether man's exploitation of the plant kingdom has always been a success story. Has it had its disasters? We have seen how some of the families containing useful plants also contain poisonous ones. Time and again we have seen how it is necessary to remove toxic or unpleasant substances before the plant could be eaten – acorns, the Californian buckeye, bistort, to mention but a few. Cassava is a staple food over much of the tropical world; how was it discovered to be edible after the highly toxic cyanide had been washed out? The hazard would have been rendered the greater by the fact that there are poisonous and non-poisonous races. And who discovered the edible properties of the tomato or the potato and brought them into cultivation? Did other highly poisonous members of this family, the Solanaceae, take their toll? Even today the deadly nightshade is a menace. Moreover, it is said to contaminate the flesh of rabbits that feed on it, though they themselves are immune to its effect. Trial and error there must have been; but one wonders how big was the error.

3

Domestic uses of wild plants

If you are reading this book sitting in the living-room of a private house, or in a library, or some such indoor setting, look round at the contents of the room and notice how much of what you see is made of materials ultimately derived from plants. Unless you are in a modern fireproof building, the likelihood is that much of what you see is of vegetable nature. The soft furnishings may be of wool or skins, though materials made from plant fibres will very likely be present too. The walls may be plaster or brick, but they may be wholly or partly of wood; and let us not forget that it used to be common practice to use chopped straw and other plant material as a component of the plaster. Much of what we see in a modern room may be of metal or of man-made material such as plastic, but in many cases these objects would have been made of wood in the days before the metal and other technologies had been developed. All this serves to show how dependent man must have been on the plant kingdom for the articles and utensils of everyday life. We shall see later (Part 2) how poorly these things are represented in the archaeological record, but reference to any work dealing with the life of existing primitive peoples will demonstrate the wide use they make of their plant environment.

No attempt can be made here to catalogue the references in the anthropological literature or in the early historical sources to the use of plant material for purposes other than food. The variation is enormous, determined by such factors as the environment (tundra, temperate forest, savanna, tropical forests, etc.) and the cultural level which the people have attained. For the present purpose it will suffice to consider some of the main categories of usage of which we have evidence from the distant past.

CONSTRUCTIONAL

Timber is by far the most widely used constructional material, and it is generally true that wherever trees were available they were used for this purpose. Where wood was scarce, other materials were used. For instance, reed houses were built in pre-dynastic Egypt, though superseded by brick or stone (Lucas, 1962). Even in wooded country the whole structure was not always of timber, and in areas where it was in short supply other materials were used instead. Walls of stone, sometimes complete stone constructions (e.g. brochs), are found in Northern Britain where timber was scarce and stone abundant. Adobe or mud-brick construction is found in arid areas, and skins may be used to construct the walls in, for instance, grasslands or the tundra. But some timbering is very often incorporated in the framework in all such cases, and such timber may be used over and over again as new buildings replace the old. Sometimes certain species are preferred: the lodgepole pine (*Pinus contorta*) gets its vernacular name from its favoured use for the framework of houses by the Indians of the western Plains. (Its botanical name *contorta* describes the twisting of the branches and is not descriptive of the growth of the main stem which is both rapid and straight.) In other situations any wood which comes to hand may be used. Some shore-dwelling peoples, for instance, utilize driftwood for constructional purposes.

We know from the number and size of postholes on archaeological sites in forested country (such as the long houses of the people who made Linear Pottery) that timber was used on a large scale and the main members were themselves of large dimensions (Piggott, 1965). Considerable inroads must have been made into the forest in the neighbourhood of settlements, and the forest dominants must have been exploited in addition to the smaller pole-size trees used for the secondary and tertiary orders of the framework construction. The very abundant remains of timber in the Swiss (Tschumi, 1949) and Italian[14] pile-dwellings show the same prodigality in the use of wood. Many species were used, presumably depending on what was easily available. On other types of site it appears that oak was usually the species used, as it continued to be for this purpose as long as timber-framed buildings were being constructed. Walls were often made of shingles or split timbers and the floors of planks or laths, perhaps covered with loam or plaster. Birch bark is recorded as flooring material and also as insulation round fireplaces and ovens.[167] It is largely a matter of speculation as to what materials would have been used for the roof, but from what we know of recent practice among the North American Indian and other primitive usages, it seems likely that the bark of certain trees would have been used, along with other plant materials that could be so arranged to shed water and exclude wind. The long sword-shaped leaves of some marsh plants (e.g. sweet flag (*Acorus*), reedmace (*Typha*) or *Cladium*), the straight stems of rushes (*Juncus*) and doubtless various tall-growing grasses could have been used much as wheat straw is used for thatching today. Incidentally, wheat straw is known in the trade as reed; true reed (*Phragmites communis*), a more lasting thatching material, goes by the name of Norfolk reed, though that county is not the exclusive source. Heather is still used for thatching in places where it is abundant, and it is likely that the roofing of houses with turf-sods, still to be found in the remoter parts of Britain or in Iceland, is an age-old practice in such places. Other places, other materials: in tropical countries, for instance, banana leaves are widely used for thatching.

In addition to the construction of the actual dwellings themselves it appears from archaeological evidence that there was often a palisade enclosing the house or farmstead, as at Little Woodbury[16] and being primarily protective, this would involve the use of smaller-sized timber in considerable quantity. Moreover, wattle hurdles are known from prehistoric sites, very similar in construction to those still made today. We cannot tell exactly how they were used but modern practice is probably a good guide.

Whereas timber as a constructional material is usually ephemeral in temperate regions, so that we have to infer its existence from such evidence as postholes, in semi-arid regions a much less destructible material, mud-brick or adobe, has been used ever since houses themselves have been built. Whilst such material is therefore largely outside the scope of this book, it is interesting to recall, as the Bible reminds us, that such bricks commonly required straw for their manufacture. Chopped straw or grass was added as a binder, particularly where the material had a lower clay content than was desirable. This improved not only the strength of the clay, but apparently its plasticity as well. Why it should do so is still not fully understood, but a clue may be obtained from the fact that clay soaked in humus-rich solutions or in peat water becomes more plastic. This may be due to the substitution of hydrogen ions on the clay colloids, so increasing the dispersion of the colloids and increasing plasticity. The silica remains of grasses have also been found in pottery, where they were presumably introduced for a similar purpose, to improve the working properties of the clay. Grass itself may have been used or the silica material could have been introduced in another form such as dung.

HOUSEHOLD

Under this heading we may consider the multifarious objects used in and about a homestead. As has already been said, a great many such objects are, or would originally have been, of plant origin, and this inevitably means that they are only exceptionally preserved. In fact, most of our knowledge of these things is indirect. For instance, the presence of loom-weights implies the presence of a loom and this would have had a timber framework. However, finds made in peatbogs and waterlogged graves in Denmark, in the desiccated tombs of the Ancient Egyptians, or in sites like the 30-m-deep shaft into the chalk at Wilsford, near Stonehenge,[7] have contributed more than the domestic sites themselves.

Wood was probably the most widely used material in the ordinary household. Not unexpectedly the wooden finds from peatbogs have largely been of implements used on the land: spades, shovels, peatcutters, handles for hoes and adzes, and even ploughs. However, more domestic articles have also been found. Spoons or ladles made of hazel, alder or oak, bowls and beakers of alder, rowan or elm, and even combs have turned up in peat bogs and lake deposits. Enough buckets have been discovered in this way to be able to show the development of construction from the primitive type – a hollowed out piece of wood – to the more sophisticated ones of stave construction, an example of which was recovered (in fragments) from the Wilsford Shaft. They are usually made of alder.

There must have been many objects in the average household that were fashioned out of wood but of which no record remains. Some glimpse of this is afforded by the finds from tombs in Ancient Egypt; toys, statuettes, models and ornate caskets have been remarkably preserved,[128] and these in a region where wood was not abundant.

Practically nothing is recorded about house furniture; this is not the sort of object which would easily find its way into a peat bog. Moreover, the constant risk of fire in the houses themselves would reduce the chances of such things being preserved elsewhere. It is reasonable to assume that there was furniture, and indeed one example of a site with domestic furniture is known from the Late Neolithic.[25] This is Skara Brae, in the Orkneys, where beds, tables and so forth were made of stone. Timber would be scarce in the Orkneys, but just as it has been suggested that pottery vessels are copies in another medium of wooden or basketwork containers (see below), so it is reasonable to assume that this furniture is a version in stone of objects usually made of timber. Similar stone fittings are known from other places, for example the Scilly Isles, where timber was also likely to have been scarce. Another source of information about furniture is the clay models known from the Neolithic of Eastern Europe (Childe, 1957).

An essential item in the household would be the box or container. We have already seen how containers can be made from birch bark in such a way that they can hold liquids; birch-bark containers are known from the Swiss pile-dwellings,[167] and similar articles are still made by the American Indians.[89] A bast-sewn box of lime bark is known from the Early Bronze Age of Denmark (Clark, 1952), and more elaborate examples are known from later periods. Nevertheless, the need for stouter boxes would still arise, and once wood-gouging tools had been devised these could be made out of the solid. Other vessels such as cups and bowls were made in this way, too. Such vessels in various stages of construction have been recovered from the Lago di Ledro, in Italy.[14] Later, as with buckets, more refined and less laborious methods of construction would be devised. Where timber was in relatively short supply other materials were used; in Ancient Egypt, for instance, leaves of papyrus (*Cyperus papyrus*) were worked around a reed framework to make boxes (Lucas, 1962).

There is some evidence that early pottery shapes were directly inspired by containers made from vegetable material which were in use before pottery was invented. An example of such skeuomorphs, as they have been called, comes from the Linear Pottery period in Eastern Europe, where pottery bowls and bottles are very reminiscent in shape of the gourd – a plant which originated in the Old World. With a little imagination some of the incised patterns on these vessels can be seen as representing the slings or nets in which the gourds were carried. This parallel, if true, raises considerable archaeological questions, for the gourd does not harden as far north as the Bakony Forest or the Carpathians where the main concentration of such pottery occurs. Was there, then, some contact, direct or indirect, with more southerly regions? Another example of pottery style based on plant materials is coiled ware, supposedly a representation of basketry, while from Denmark come two vessels made of elm and rowan wood whose shape closely resembles that of funnel-beakers, suggesting that they may be wooden precursors of that pottery form.[161]

Pottery and plant material were associated in a different way in the Cortaillod ware of the Swiss Neolithic. Birch-bark patterns were glued on to the outside of the pots with wood pitch to give a characteristic form of decoration. Combs have also been found with the grip similarly treated.[167]

Papyrus itself is not pliable enough to be woven, but many other plant stems and leaves can be woven or plaited and this made possible the construction of a wide range of household chattels. Inevitably remains of such articles are much more numerous in semi-arid areas. Our concern here is the plants that were used rather than the actual techniques and applications of basketry, matting and the weaving of plant fibres. The Egyptian remains show that a great variety of plants was used; reeds, sedges, palm fibres, flax and a number of grasses. The sea-rush, *Juncus maritimus*, a widespread plant of coastal regions, was a particularly useful plant for this and other purposes (Lucas, 1962).

Apart from the naturally-occurring plants whose leaves and stems could be used directly for the preparation of materials, there is the large group of plants from which fibres could be extracted. The fine fibres could be spun into threads or into more massive forms of cordage such as ropes. Many of the plants already mentioned could also provide fibres when suitably treated. The processing usually consisted of soaking the stems or leaves so that partial decomposition disorganized the non-fibrous tissue (retting) and then beating the material until the fibres were separated from the matrix tissue. Then they could be used directly, or more usually spun into yarn or cord. In Ancient Egypt reed (*Phragmites communis*) – also a widespread plant of temperate regions – esparto grass (*Stipa tenacissima*), halfa grass (*Desmostachya bipinnata*), papyrus and especially palm fibre were important sources of cordage (Lucas, 1962). As usual our knowledge of what plants were used in north-western Europe is less complete, but as just indicated, reed was available, and in addition the more extensive forest cover provided a source of fibre in the trees. Archaeological literature is full of references to bast fibres, indicating that the fibres are of vegetable origin, but more detailed identification is seldom made. This is due to the belief that such fibres have little specific character (see p. 132). Bast fibres have been produced from a variety of trees, e.g. lime, elm, birch, willow and even cedar, but by far the most important of these in Europe is lime (Hodges, 1964). Even up to recent times lime bast has been an important material, in spite of the fact that lime trees are now much less abundant than they were in prehistoric times. Nor is its usefulness confined to human need. I have watched jackdaws tearing strips of bark several feet long from the dead branches of a lime tree. The strips were then carried away to a nearby house and stuffed down the chimney as nesting material. On the whole tree fibres tend to be rather coarse, more suitable for cordage than for weaving. Herbaceous plants provide finer fibres. The stinging nettle – which we regard as a weed – has already been mentioned as a source of food, and in addition it was, and has been until quite recently, a valuable source of fine fibre. Another plant, *Polytrichum commune*, the hair moss, also provided a fine fibre used in prehistoric times for clothing and other purposes (Clark, 1952). This moss is commonly found – especially after a fire – in acid wet places, which must have become more frequent as the forest was driven back, a striking example of how man's needs could be met by widely different types of vegetation.

Before leaving the subject of fibres and particularly cordage, mention should be made of the practice of the North American Indian of using tree roots for coarse sewing and binding (Driver, 1964; Yarnell, 1964). Certain trees, when growing on poor soil, will send out shallow roots which run straight and almost unbranched for many yards. They are easily accessible, especially if running just beneath a layer of raw humus, and would have a multitude of uses. No prehistoric evidence of such a use is known from Europe, yet pine and birch commonly behave in this way on heathland soils. The sources of fibre used by the North American Indians are very similar to those already mentioned here: trees, especially lime and elm, nettles, water-plants and a number of other herbs.

Cultivation of fibre plants such as hemp, flax and cotton reduced the dependence on wild sources and produced fibres more suitable for man's needs. Nevertheless the use of wild sources still continued, especially in the more remote areas and for special purposes, and has done so up to the present day.

Sewing with the finer threads called for the use of needles. Needles made of bone and antler are well known from the prehistoric periods and were doubtless the most widely used form, but it is noteworthy that the North American Indians also used long thorns (Yarnell, 1964). Thorn bushes are familiar plants in most regions and would provide a readily available source of needles which could be regarded as expendable. They would be much less durable than bone or antler needles and would rarely be preserved in domestic sites.

47

A material of vegetable origin which perhaps ought to be mentioned is bark cloth, a product apparently of great antiquity in the Pacific Islands and also in Africa. In the Pacific it is made direct from the bark of a tree of the mulberry family, *Broussonetia papyrifera*, which is stripped off in sheets. After soaking and beating, the under-bark fibres are freed from the outer bark and are then further beaten to the required thickness. It is possible to join several sheets merely by beating the edges together, the natural gums in the tissue holding them together. Today this plant is cultivated for the purpose, for example in Fiji. It is not allowed to reach large size, however, but is stripped when the stems are little more than wands. The narrow strips of tissue are beaten together, and cassava starch is added as an adhesive. Nevertheless, even from such small sections lengths of over 30 m of material are made for ceremonial purposes. In the Caribbean bark cloth was used as the wrapping for 'cigarettes' – as distinct from cigars which were wrapped in tobacco leaves (Driver, 1964). Perhaps this is no more than an interesting digression, for such material is unlikely to persist in archaeological deposits; for one thing, by the very nature of its manufacture, it will disintegrate if subjected to prolonged wetting.

If this has been a digression at least it serves as a link between fabrics and another material of unquestionable archaeological importance, papyrus. This was made in a very similar manner to bark cloth, thin strips of pith being laid edge to edge and overlain by another layer with the strips at right angles to the first. They were then beaten together, and again the natural adhesive in the pith caused them to adhere together as a sheet. For larger sheets wheat starch was added as an adhesive. The longest known continuous length of papyrus is 40 m.[128] A similar principle also operated in the early forms of paper making. In Ancient Egypt linen and wood, as well as papyrus, were used for writing on, and the pen, too, was of vegetable origin. In its earliest form it consisted of a stem of the rush *Juncus maritimus*, frayed at one end to produce a fringe of 'bristles', so that it could be used to make either a thin or a broad line (Lucas, 1962). Later, from Graeco-Roman times onward, this was superseded by reed stems (*Phragmites*) which were shaped and split in much the same way as a quill pen. The early inks were mostly based on carbon-black, though galls (tannins) were used in Egypt from about 400 B.C. Recently a large number of thin wooden tablets, some still carrying decipherable writing in carbon-based ink, have been found at the Roman fort of Vindolanda on Hadrian's Wall.[142]

This brings us to the subject of tanning; if writing was not really a domestic occupation, tanning certainly was, and for its effect it was very largely dependent upon plants from the countryside. The preparation of leather probably goes back to the Palaeolithic, but in Europe no evidence is known earlier than the late Neolithic. Chemically tannins are complex and diverse, but for our purpose here they may be divided into two main groups, the pyrogallol and the catechol groups. Both have an irreversible effect on skins which prevents or at least slows down their decomposition by bacteria. Tannins of the pyrogallol group are obtained, for instance, from the wood of chestnut and oak, the leaves of sumac, the fruit of myrobalanus, and oak galls (Clark, 1952; Hodges, 1964; Lucas, 1962). These tannins produced a pale-coloured leather. Catechol tannins come from the woods of mimosa, mangrove, pine, and the bark of larch, and they give a more solid leather with a pink to reddish colour. Some materials contain tannins of both types: oak and hemlock (*Tsuga*) bark are examples. Oak was the main source of tannin in Western Europe right up to the fifteenth century when sumac was introduced from the Near East. It is interesting to note that the oak galls (oak apples – not fruits, but galls produced by a parasitic insect larva) contain even more tannin than oak bark and were valued for this purpose. Even the true fruits of the oak, the acorns, contain tannin, and we have already seen that it was normal practice to leach this out before the acorns were used as food. Again there is an example of a plant of the open country being used for the same purpose as a forest tree: even in the last few centuries the roots of the little herb tormentil (*Potentilla erecta*) have been used for dressing leather (Clark, 1952). This plant is widespread, occurring in rich pastures and on acid mountain soils, on chalk downs and in acid bogs. That such a use should have been found for such an insignificant plant shows how familiar men were with the plants of their environment and underlines their dependence upon them.

We have already seen how starch can be used as an adhesive in making bark cloth or papyrus, and even today the older generation is familiar with flour paste and realizes that not all adhesives come out of glossy coloured tubes bearing mysterious names. Glues, in the particular sense, are made from animal materials and are therefore outside the scope of this book, but gums and resins are of vegetable origin and were widely used in antiquity. Both gums and resins are secreted by plants in the form in which they are useful to man and consequently need no preparation apart, perhaps, from purification. Gums are carbohydrates – chemically related to sugars and starches – and are miscible with water, the sticking properties developing as they dry out. They may be obtained from a wide variety of plants, among which acacias (one acacia produces the well-known gum arabic) are of outstanding importance (Lucas, 1962). In Ancient Egypt there was a long history of the use of gums derived from various acacias. In places where suitable gum plants are not available an alternative source may lie in mucilaginous plants such as lichens or seaweeds; mucilages are merely watered-down gums and if dried out would serve similar purposes.

Resins, on the other hand, are not miscible with water. They are secreted by the plants as solutions in essential oils, and as the oils evaporate the resin hardens. They are most commonly obtained from coniferous trees, pine, larch and fir being the main sources in Europe, though some non-coniferous species also produce resins (Lucas, 1962). Some conifers only produce resin when they are wounded, others have a permanent system of resin canals throughout the plant. The secretion serves to heal wounds and is also thought to have certain bactericidal and fungicidal properties. The water-resistance of resin may also be useful to the plant to conserve moisture, as in the 'sticky buds' of the horse chestnut (*Aesculus hippocastanum*) or the balsam poplar (*Populus gileadensis*).

Wood pitch or wood tar, also of a resinous nature, can be distilled from wood. This was done by the Greeks as far back as the 4th century B.C., though they probably did not understand the principle of the process. Wood pitch was also widely used by the North American Indian for caulking canoes and making watertight containers.

The important difference between gums and resinous substances in their relation to water determined the use to which they were put. Gums were useless for outdoor work; thus we see resin being used, for instance, to set the flints into the wooden hafts of sickles (Clark, 1962). They could also be mixed with a mineral base to prepare a cement which would be weather-resistant. A special application of resins is in the preparation of varnish. Much research has gone into the difficult problem of identifying the sources of varnishes used in Ancient Egypt (Lucas, 1962). It appears that certain kinds of resin were dissolved in a drying oil (e.g. linseed or hempseed oil) to produce a lasting varnish.

CLOTHING

Through most of prehistoric time animal materials have provided man's clothing, especially in the northern latitudes where wind-protection and warmth were of paramount importance. Vegetable materials are relatively rare and then they are usually prepared from plants cultivated for their fibres, such as flax or hemp. There are few records of the use of wild plants. Tree bark was probably used as footwear, though leather shoes date back to the Bronze Age and were no doubt a more comfortable and satisfactory article. In arid areas sandals were made from plant materials. They are among the most frequent plant artefacts found in archaeological sites of the arid regions of North America (Driver, 1964), and there is a parallel in Ancient Egypt where sandals were made of reed or papyrus.[128] At the other extreme hair-nets have been found made of bast fibres, and an unfinished article made of hair moss was found in a fort-ditch in Southern Scotland, dated about A.D. 80 (Clark, 1952). However, since this has been interpreted variously as a cap or a bag, it does not contribute much to our catalogue of clothing derived from wild plants.

Perhaps the greatest contribution of wild plants to dress was in the matter of dyes and colouring. Nearly all natural dyes are of plant origin. In the British flora there are about 100 wild plants which even today are used as a source of vegetable dyes by those interested in handicrafts.[159] To mention but a few, according to the colour they produce:

Yellow : Barberry (*Berberis vulgaris*) – stem or root.
Bracken (*Pteridium aquilinum*) – rhizome.
Heather (*Calluna vulgaris*) – flowering shoots.
Pine (*Pinus sylvestris*) – cones.
Pear (*Pyrus communis*) – leaves.
Gorse (*Ulex europaeus*) – bark, flowers and young shoots.

Green : Privet (*Ligustrum vulgare*) – berries.
Reed (*Phragmites communis*) – flower heads.
Dyer's Greenweed (*Genista tinctoria*) – whole plant. When used alone this plant gives a yellow colour, but it gets its name from its former use with woad (see below) to produce green.

Brown : Birch (*Betula pendula*) – bark.
Juniper (*Juniperus communis*) – berries.
Onion (*Allium*) – outer skin of bulb.

Black :	Elder (*Sambucus nigra*) – bark.
	Meadow Sweet (*Filipendula ulmaria*) – root.
Red :	Bedstraw (*Galium boreale*) – root.
	Dandelion (*Taraxacum officinale*) – root.
	St John's Wort (*Hypericum*) – flower heads.
Blue :	Dog's Mercury (*Mercurialis perennis*) – whole plant.
	Alder buckthorn (*Frangula alnus*) – berries.
	Bilberry (*Vaccinium myrtillus*) – berries.

These colours can often be altered considerably by using various mordants such as iron, alum, chrome or tin. It is not possible to say whether such techniques were known to prehistoric man, but it is not beyond the bounds of possibility, especially once he became knowledgeable about the uses of the metal ores.

This short section would not be complete without the mention of woad (*Isatis tinctoria*) – the only prehistoric colouring matter known, by name at least, to all schoolchildren. It was cultivated in the Roman Iron Age (Clark, 1952) and continued as a crop in East Anglia until 1924, when it finally had to give way to imported indigo. Today it is a rare plant, one of its few stations being at the confluence of the Severn and the Avon at Tewkesbury, and there must remain some doubt as to whether it is truly wild or an escape from early cultivation.

FUEL

The perpetual demand for fuel, for fires for warmth, cooking, protection, pottery making and for ritual purposes, has been the basis of man's greatest impact on the vegetation of the surrounding countryside. Indeed there is a peculiar paradox between man's widespread practice of burning the countryside, whether by design or accident, and the need to conserve a supply of fuel near at hand. Some prehistoric sites of the Plains Indians appear to have been evacuated after only short occupation, supposedly due to the exhaustion of firewood in the vicinity,[67] an exhaustion of resources that might well have been aggravated by uncontrolled burning. Even today a great deal of energy and time may be expended by rural people in collecting firewood from far afield, particularly where human transport is the only sort available. I am reminded of the American, visiting one of the deforested countries of the Near East, who saw a woman staggering along under a huge bundle of firewood, preceded by her overweight husband riding empty-handed on an ass. Outraged by this indignity to womanhood he stopped the man and asked why he was riding while his overburdened wife had to walk. Mystified, the man answered, 'But my wife hasn't got a donkey.' Perhaps the moral of this is irrelevant to our subject, but it shows that even with assisted transport the process may not necessarily be speeded up.

Much has been written about the fuels used by man and their suitability for different purposes (Hodges, 1964). Here suffice to say that early man would be well aware of the burning properties of different woods; that some need to be dried out, whilst others can be burnt green. As today among primitive peoples, so doubtless it has always been, dead wood is preferred to sappy living wood, because it gives a quicker and hotter fire, and this probably led to the cutting and storage of wood in addition to the collecting of dead wood. Different woods may have been used according to the purpose of the fire, whether it was newly lit or was required to smoulder until needed again. The forest Indian in North America may damp a fire down until his return by covering it with turves, this in an area where the trees are mostly rapid-burning conifers.[101] In deciduous-forest country elm or poplar may have been used to keep the fire alive but quiet. For many purposes, however, it seems that indiscriminate use of species was made, judging by the mixed composition of charcoal samples from prehistoric sites.

The practice of making charcoal is an ancient one, certainly known in the later prehistoric periods. It was presumably understood that charcoal gave a much higher temperature than wood, since energy was not used in evaporating moisture and other volatiles, and converting the carbohydrates into carbon. Charcoal was therefore of particular value for metal-smelting. It would be a matter of some interest to be able to deduce whether a hearth was the site of a charcoal or a wood fire, but as either will leave fragments of charcoal in the ashes it is not possible to decide with certainty. However, it has struck me, when analysing charcoal samples submitted from archaeological sites that some contain a great variety of species, including bushes such as broom (*Sarothamnus*), thorns (e.g. blackthorn (*Prunus spinosa*) and hawthorn), and shrubs such as hazel, as well as remains of forest timbers such as ash and oak, whilst others are purely of one species, usually oak or hazel. If there is any evidence that oak or hazel were the favoured species in charcoal-burning, we might be seeing the difference between a general-purpose fire on the one hand and a charcoal fire on the other. Unfortunately the sites of old charcoal-kilns are difficult to identify, and until more data are available on the practice in ancient times the question must remain open.

Though by far the most important, wood is not the only fuel used in antiquity. In regions where wood was naturally scarce, or had become so through human activity, peat, dung and even coal are known to have been used, as indeed they are today. In such areas wood is still preferred if it can be obtained; the Eskimo, for instance, will travel long distances to collect driftwood, but if driven to it he will turn to ericaceous shrubs as a substitute. There are also records of the use of reeds and grasses, and even today leaf-litter and humus may be collected from the forest as fuel, a practice very damaging to the fertility of the forest soil.

Other inflammable materials were used incidentally. Floor coverings of rushes or bracken may well have been burnt; likewise the turves removed from the field in the process of paring and burning may have been used on domestic fires. Weeds, straw and chaff from the fields were also commonly burnt in this way.

In a primitive society it was often difficult to create fire, so there was the tendency to conserve it. One method of doing this has persisted from antiquity until the present day, namely tinder. Tinder is usually the dried fructifications of the bracket fungus *fomes fomentarios* which grows parsitically on trees. When lighted this material smoulders for a long time and can be fanned to a flame when applied to dried twigs or leaves.

In addition to heat ancient man also required light. The earliest artificial light was doubtless that provided by the fires themselves, but as far back as the palaeolithic man was making special devices for lighting. A direct extension of the fire would be the use of splinters of wood, particularly resinous wood, which could be carried about (Clark, 1952), and a development of this would be torches of rolled birch bark and similar materials, known from mesolithic times and persisting to the present day among the North American Indians. In Ancient Greece bundles of sticks of resinous wood were tied together with rushes, papyrus or vine tendrils and treated with rosin, pitch or wax to make torches.[51] The use of fats and oils as fuel for lighting also dates back to the Palaeolithic; animal fats were readily available and wicks were made from reeds or moss. Later on in the Neolithic, the products of cultivated plants such as flax or Gold of Pleasure (*Camelina sativa*) began to become available, so that in addition to animal fats and oils we find linseed oil being used with wicks of flax or hemp. In Iceland the cottony perianths of fruiting cotton-grass (*Eriopho-*

rum) were used to make wicks for use in shallow whale-oil lamps.[138] The rush-light is a primitive form of lighting which seems to be of ancient lineage but which persisted in rural areas of Britain until quite recent times. This was made from the peeled stems of the common soft rush (*Juncus effusus*) which were dipped in fat to produce a sort of taper. In the Far East wax suitable for lighting was obtained from the seeds of certain trees, notably *Rhus succedanea* in Japan, and the Tallow-tree (*Sapium sebiferum*) in China.[51]

Through Classical times and since there has been an elaboration of the many types of lamps, candles and tapers, often connected with ritual ceremonies. There was a proliferation of the substances used, the most important from our point of view being the introduction of olive oil as a fuel. Castor oil, too, was used in this way in Ancient Egypt, a use of this substance which many of us will think preferable to its modern medicinal application.

MUSICAL INSTRUMENTS

The archaeological record contains little direct evidence of musical instruments, for the simple reason that they were mostly constructed of wood or other plant material and consequently have not survived. (We must leave out of account the metal instruments such as lurs and trumpets.) The rhythm and percussion section of the orchestra were no doubt strongly represented, and we can see from the American Indian of today how such instruments would often not be recognizable as such; wooden containers or gourds containing pebbles or seeds would serve as rattles, and logs, planks or boxes were beaten as percussion instruments (Driver, 1964). Pipes and reed instruments were made from hollow stems such as bamboo. There are occasional finds of ancient stringed instruments. Designs were very varied, often with no modern parallel – as we can tell from the written record in the Bible or the painted record from Ancient Egypt – but whether they were basically harps or lutes, the framework and sounding box would be of wood and seldom preserved. An exceptional case was the two instruments preserved in the deep-freeze of the Pazyryk tombs in the Altai mountains,[123] and less perfect examples come from dry climates.

4

The use of wild plants outside the homestead

In this chapter we have to consider the contribution of the plant environment to man's activities further afield; to his transport and movement across country, to his wresting of a livelihood from the land and to his fighting against his enemies. In most of these things it is the use of wood which is important, though materials of mechanical purpose occasionally come from other plants too.

TRANSPORT

(a) By Land

Man's movement over the earth's surface involved three primary media: land, water and snow. Each demanded a different solution, and in each case the necessary materials were obtained from the environment.

In dealing with land transport we can leave out any reference to the controversial subject of horse-riding because this involved as far as we know, little use of products of the natural vegetation. The practice of bedecking horses is apparently an ancient one, for a number of finds have been made of ornamental fittings to the harness. These are usually of bone or antler, but wooden cheek-pieces and bridle ornaments are known from the 4th century B.C. (Clark, 1952). But man did invent the wheel, opening up enormous possibilities for more rapid movement of himself and his goods; and the wheel until very recent times was made of wood. The earliest wheels were merely wooden discs, shaped from one, or more usually two or three pieces dowelled together, but the spoked wheel did not lag far behind, and the two types developed side by side. A rock-painting from Spain shows both occurring in the same vehicle (Clark, 1952), and, of course, both disc and spoked wheels have persisted to the present day. As is to be expected, our best evidence on this subject comes from the dry climate of Egypt and from wheels preserved in peat bogs in the north. Unfortunately the latter often have not been dated. In Ancient Egypt elm wood was the usual material for wheels and it is remarkable that even today the wheelwright uses elm for this purpose (Lucas, 1962). Yet though elm was widely distributed through the deciduous forests of Europe in prehistoric times, the solid wheels which have been recovered from bogs were usually of oak or alder (Clark, 1952). The largest number of finds has been in Holland, where oak was almost invariably used.[168] Elsewhere, alder was more widely used than oak. To us alder would seem an odd choice since it is so soft, but we must remember that metalled roads did not exist, and wear would be much less on dirt tracks.

Though wheels are not infrequently met with in a prehistoric context, the carts or wagons which they supported are rarely found, but our best evidence of what the earliest ones looked like comes from clay models – probably children's toys – found in Eastern and Central Europe.[126] Both four-wheeled wagons and two-wheeled carts were used, the earliest record in Europe being about 3000 B.C., and their use spread across Europe, perhaps reaching Britain a few centuries later.

Perhaps better known than these rather nebulous general-purpose vehicles are the special-purpose ones such as hearses and chariots which appear in Celtic burials, but we have little information on their construction from the botanical standpoint. However, ash, elm, maple, acacia, and willow have been identified from XVIIIth Dynasty chariots in Egypt, and plum wood was identified from the spokes of one of these (Lucas, 1962). It might appear, therefore, that the choice of species was not the first criterion, though if so it is remarkable that some of these woods, such as elm, ash and maple, are not native to Egypt. The magnificent votive wagon found in a bog at Dejbjerg in Denmark shows similar botanical complexity, the wheel hubs being oak, the spokes hornbeam and the felloes made out of single pieces of ash (Clark, 1952); but here the choice in each case would be quite justified on functional grounds.

Overland transport must have presented many problems, particularly in the damper climates. This is no doubt why prehistoric trackways so often followed the upland ridges, especially where the soil was lighter. But it was not always possible to do so and marshy ground had to be crossed. In these circumstances trackways were sometimes constructed across the wettest portions, consisting of timber foundations resting on the peat. Good examples have been described in detail from Germany, Holland and the Somerset levels.[126] There are two types of such trackways. The simplest, though not always the earliest, consists of longitudinally arranged poles, usually of alder, birch, pine or hazel, laid on a bed of brushwood or heather and pegged in place. This type would clearly be useless for wheeled vehicles. The second type has a surface of transversely laid timbers, either split or in the round, and usually of alder, birch or oak. They are laid on longitudinally running poles of alder or birch, themselves laid on a brushwood foundation, the whole being pegged down with stakes.[126] Such construction is much more ambitious and would involve great expenditure of labour and materials, so we must assume that it would be a major artery of traffic. In itself it is not proof of wheeled traffic, for it would also assist sled transport, but the discovery of wheels in the vicinity of such trackways is significant.

Finally we must mention that aspect of land transport which everyone has wondered about: the transport of massive blocks of stone such as the trilithons of Stonehenge, or the huge blocks of the pyramids. The use of rollers seems the only possible answer, though we have no direct evidence. To carry out such an operation over even reasonably even ground would require large-size timbers, and the wastage by damage must have been considerable. The problem of finding such timber would be quite daunting on Salisbury Plain in the Bronze Age; it must have been more difficult in Egypt, never a land of big trees.

(b) By Water

Movement by water has been important ever since man sought his livelihood along the water's edge, whether sea, lake or river. Water was at one and the same time his easiest means of movement, especially when the forest was dense and undisturbed, and his source of food. The earliest form of boat one would expect to be a skin or bark shell built around a framework, similar to the canoes used by the North American Indians and the Eskimos today, but with one exception there is no record of such a craft from antiquity. The one exception is an undated boat from Sweden; it was built from a single sheet of spruce bark sewn to a wooden framework (Clark, 1952). Other forms of craft involving a minimum of technical knowledge were probably constructed from reeds; such boats are used even today by people dwelling in extensive swamps, and similar craft built of papyrus were used in Ancient Egypt.[128] Strangely enough, there seems to be no evidence of rafts built from heavier materials such as timber.

We tend to think of the dug-out as a most primitive type, but in fact it could not be made until man had developed stone or flint axes capable of felling a large tree and hollowing out the trunk. This would involve excavating most of the heartwood, a formidable proposition with a tree such as oak. The necessary technology was not achieved until the Mesolithic, but once achieved the construction of dug-out boats spread widely through Europe. A similar story no doubt held good in many other regions; even today the Indians of the Pacific coast of North America have strong preferences in the selection of trees for making such boats. The great majority of prehistoric boats found in Europe have been made of oak, but as Clark (1952) has pointed out this may be a reflection of the relative resistance of oak to decay. This suggestion is supported by the fact that at Aamosen in Denmark fifteen boats made out of alder were found and others are known made from elm, poplar, Scots pine and silver fir. This list makes the point that the manufacture of dug-out boats was common to both the coniferous and deciduous type of forest, and also that among these timbers were a number that were much easier to work than oak. The North American Indian today uses basswood (*Tilia americana*) for this purpose (Yarnell, 1964). The criterion of choice may well have been the form of the tree rather than the species, a long, straight and branch-free bole being the first consideration, and this is as much a matter of the conditions under which the tree grew as of the species itself. A tree growing in the open, such as a park specimen, will have branches low down on the trunk; the clean straight bole is found in trees growing in closed canopy so that lateral light does not reach the stems. Thus relatively undisturbed forest is necessary to produce trees which are old enough and straight enough for this purpose. Judging by the trees we see today it is difficult to visualize the potential of some of our common forest species. A few years ago there was a magnificent specimen of sessile oak (*Quercus petraea*) in Whitley Wood in the New Forest which rivalled in form and size many a tropical aristocrat. It was too good to live and has now been 'converted' into lumber – and, no doubt, cash. Our present heritage consists of badly grown and often genetically undesirable stock; the choice trees have been removed and the poor ones left to breed. Even our traditional relic giants are no guide as to what a good tree looks like. The Knightwood oak, for example, was pollarded early in life, so that its form was ruined; and the Major Oak, in Sherwood Forest, like many of the living skeletons in our villages, is so coarsely branched at low level that it is likely to have grown in open conditions or in a clearing rather than in dense forest. However, we must remember that the tall straight tree was not always the ideal. In the days of the oaken walls of the British Navy oaks with heavy curved side branches were fashionable since they provided the ribs of the ships with little need for shaping. In those days the forests (e.g. the Forest of Dean) were managed with a view to producing such trees.[65]

It is not our purpose here to discuss the development of boat forms through the prehistoric period, but as the form changed from the dug-out to the plank-built boat, the need for long straight lengths of wood remained the same. Oak seems to have been used almost exclusively in the more advanced forms of hull construction in Europe (though a prehistoric war canoe built of lime planks is known from Denmark (Clark, 1952)), but other materials played a subsidiary part. The Ferriby boats, for instance, showed a plank construction, oak planks being sewn together with yew withes and the seams caulked with moss.[181] Three species of moss were used, caulking rope was made from *Polytrichum commune* (hair moss) and wadding from *Neckera complanata* and *Eurhynchium striatum*. Elsewhere seaweed was used for caulking; the hygroscopic properties of the mucilaginous seaweed prevented the seams drying out even when the boat was out of the water.

The accoutrements of an operational boat, the paddles and the rudder (a late development), were also made of wood, though our information on the species used is scanty. If there was a sail, the mast would be a wooden spar, though the sail itself was usually skins or leather. However, rock carvings are known which appear to show a small tree in place of the mast and sail.[98] This seems to be a ritual procedure which has parallels in much more recent times. A dug-out canoe discovered in Sussex in 1858[1] was lying upside down near a large mass – a cartload – of well-preserved 'brambles, gorse, thorn and hazel', perhaps the cargo which capsized it. This canoe had a wooden anchor shaped like a double-fluked metal one. The wood used was yew, which although one of our densest woods, nevertheless floats. Presumably it was weighted in some way, perhaps with stones.

(c) Over Snow and Ice

Finally, under the heading of transport a little needs to be said about movement over ice and snow. Skis, sledges and skates are all ancient devices, known from prehistoric times. Again we are not concerned with the detail and development of these things, but only with the use made of plants in their construction. Skates we can leave out, since they were generally made from long-bones, but skis were made of wood, as also the runners of the sledges. The superstructures of sledges are nearly always missing, so we can only surmise what they looked like and what they were made of.

By the nature of things, skis and sledges are required only in regions of prolonged snow, that is, in regions where the trees are mainly coniferous, so it is not surprising that in Europe skis and the runners of sledges were made of pine or occasionally of spruce.[80] In North America the Indians favour one or other of the species of ash for sled runners (Yarnell, 1964), but these would not have been generally available in the coniferous forest belt. In Scandinavia skis were almost invariably of pine, though two examples are known made of oak; both these, significantly, came from the southern margin of the coniferous belt in Scandinavia where it merges into the deciduous forest zone (Clark, 1952). The compression wood of pine, from the underside of lateral branches, was most favoured (Clark, 1952). This would have naturally built-in curvature, as well as being relatively easy to work through having wide-spaced rings (in contrast to the hardwoods).

WARFARE AND HUNTING

It is not always easy to separate these two uses, since what will kill an animal will usually kill a man equally well. There are, of course, exceptions: a harpoon is not designed to hasten human demise, whereas, on the other hand, a sword is. Spears and bows and arrows, however, may be equally useful for both purposes, and in the archaeological setting it is sometimes difficult to decide which a find represents. The use of these weapons dates back, as we know from rock paintings, to the Palaeolithic, and one case is known of a wooden spear embedded in the ribs of a mammoth. Bows and arrows are known in quite good states of preservation from the Neolithic onwards, spears perhaps less so (Clark, 1952). As usual with wooden objects, preservation in the peat bogs of the north has been our most profitable source of finds, though these are not always well dated. Living as we do in the post-Robin Hood era, we think of bows being made only of yew wood, and it is true that this tradition goes back into the past. Yew bows of neolithic age have been recovered from the Somerset levels and the Fens of East Anglia.[28] But other woods can also be used. Bows made of elm wood have been found in Danish bogs – one more service to man rendered by this species – and one of pine is known from Sweden. In North America hickory (*Carya ovata*) was used by the Indians for both bows and arrows, and the same is true of several species of ash (Yarnell, 1964). Arrow shafts made of ash have also been recovered from Danish bogs, though in northern Europe pine was the most frequent. Other species were also used,[28] such as alder, *Viburnum* and yew. The remains of a shaft embedded in a bronze arrowhead from Motya in Sicily also proved to be of yew.[79] In places where woody plants are scarce, reed stems have been used as arrow shafts. It seems, therefore, that there is greater variety in the materials used for arrows than in those used for bows. Nevertheless the qualities necessary for a bow are not confined to yew and elm, and we may expect finds of other species, particularly ash, to come to light one day.

Arrow shafts were sometimes merely pointed, sometimes bolt-headed – that is, having an enlarged end for stunning birds and small animals without damaging the skins (Clark, 1952). But more usually some sort of arrowhead was attached, both for hunting purposes and for warfare. Such heads, typically of flint and later of metals, were commonly attached to the shaft with resin or birch tar, though this was not so necessary with socketed arrowheads of metal.

There is no evidence from the archaeological record of the use of poisoned arrows, though it may be assumed that where suitable poisons are to be found they would be known about and used. Most of such poisons are of vegetable origin, and they must be of such a nature that they do not render the prey unfit for human consumption; this consideration might not be so important where the victim is a fellow human being. Wooden throwing sticks, very similar to the Australian boomerang, have been found in the Neolithic of Switzerland (Tschumi, 1949) and in Britain. They, too, could be used for either hunting or warfare.

The club is another weapon which could be used against man or beast; it does not require very special properties, apart from shape and size, but a wood which splits easily would clearly be a disadvantage. The North American Indians find the black gum (*Nyssa sylvatica*) ideal for the purpose (Yarnell, 1964). One of the finds at Ehenside Tarn referred to earlier, was in all probability a wooden club.[31] In spite of the cartoonists' favourite picture of palaeolithic man slaying a dinosaur with a nail-studded club, we have no direct evidence of this weapon in antiquity.

Turning to defence, as opposed to attack, the shield was useful as a defence against one's human enemies, but of limited value in hunting. The material used varied according to the place and the age; hide or leather,

wood and metal. Usually the wood, if that were used, has gone, but sometimes, as at Sutton Hoo, we are left with the metal bosses which adorned
the shield.[20]

Whilst on the subject of defence let us remember defensive earthworks,
culminating in the huge hill forts of the Iron Age. Timber was often used
in these on a large scale: for palisades, bulwarks, revetments, massive
doors (as evidenced by the great stones on which they pivoted) and
various other buildings associated with the fort. Some idea of the prodigal
use of timber in this way is given by the Early Iron Age fortified village at
Biskupin, Poland, well illustrated in Piggott's *Ancient Europe* (1965) and
by Kostrewski.[97] This particular fort is on a river promontory and therefore probably in wooded country, but frequently Iron Age forts – so-
called hill forts – are sited on hills which were treeless (though pollen
analysis proves that some were in wooded country), and the supply of
timber must have been a real problem.

An object which had a wide distribution in the Bronze Age and after
was the tread-trap (Clark, 1952). It consists of a heavy oak frame (a
willow one is known from Denmark) with a horizontal flap, usually also of
oak though birch has been recorded, held in position by pegged-back
springs of a pliable wood such as hazel, willow or beech. For long these
objects were completely misinterpreted, being variously identified as
musical instruments, machines for making peat-bricks, model boats and
devices for catching pike. True, most of these theories took account of the
fact that the objects were usually found near rivers or lakes (the musical
instrument theory brings idyllic pictures to the imagination), but it is now
known that they are in fact tread-traps; an animal stepping on the flap
released the spring and became caught by the foot. In fact versions of this
device still in use today have been found in Poland, where they are set in
wet places where animals come to drink.

Here we may also mention the use of nets for fishing and possibly also
for taking gregarious birds such as seabirds. Nets are occasionally found
dating back to prehistoric times, the oldest known fragment being of
Maglemosian date. Such early nets are usually made of plant material such
as willow bast or more usually of lime bast once the lime tree had established itself in the Post-glacial sequence. Some primitive peoples even
today treat their nets with various herbal extracts which are supposed to
attract fish, a practice which probably has an old foundation.

A more certain way of ensuring success is the use of fish poisons such as
derris, obtained from the roots of various species of the tropical genus

Derris. The fish are stunned or killed outright, so that they only have to be collected as they float to the surface. In California the cyanide extracted from the seed of the buckeye (see p. 35) was used as a fish poison by the Indians (Driver, 1964). Today some individuals of *Homo sapiens* use a much less sophisticated method of achieving the same end – namely explosives.

Among the odd collection of implements from Ehenside Tarn were two peculiar objects reasonably interpreted as eel-spears. They were made of oak. When the tarn was drained last century it was found to be full of carp and eels, and the bodies of eels were found embedded in the peat during subsequent workings.[31]

Another hunting technique practised by the North American Indians is the smoking of certain plants in the belief that this attracts deer (Yarnell, 1964). A wide variety of plants is used in this way: the flowers of swamp persicaria (*Polygonum coccineum*), the seeds of bristly crowfoot (*Ranunculus pensylvanicus*), the bark of hawthorn (*Crataegus* spp.), the root of the starflower (*Trientalis borealis*), to mention only a few. With wooden pipes there would be little trace of this practice for the archaeologist to pick up, but one day someone may make a study of the botany of prehistoric pipe-dottle.

For the sake of completeness perhaps we ought to mention, in connection with warfare, the use of war-canoes and war-chariots. This is merely a different usage of forms of transportation already discussed, and holds no particular botanical interest. In concluding this section, however, it is well to remember that one of the biggest items of defence was the forest itself. This is shown by the discontinuous courses of defensive earthworks such as Offa's Dyke. Breaks occur in the line for no reason now apparent, and it has been reasonably suggested that at the time these defences were in use blocks of forest occupied the blank stretches. No further defence was necessary.

MINING

This subject calls for brief mention for two reasons. First, a good deal of timber was necessary both for underground staging and for fuel. The mineral lodes were commonly worked by fire-setting;[127] that is, heating up the rock and allowing it to cool, so that differential expansion and contraction caused the lode to crack or even fall away from the rock. Clearly this called for a large and continuing supply of fuel. It has been calculated that about 9 unit volumes of wood would be required to release one unit volume of mineral ore (Clark, 1952). The demand on the surrounding countryside would be for quantity rather than quality, so that complete forest clearance probably occurred. Wood was also used for lighting in the galleries; torches of burning wood chips, probably of resinous species, were apparently used, an age-old practice, as we have seen. This would not make great demands on the fuel resources, but the same could not be said of the need for fuel for the smelting process, often carried out just outside the mine adit.

The second point of importance with regard to prehistoric mining will be discussed more appropriately in Chapter 7 but should be mentioned here. It is remarkable that a rich collection of perishable objects is recovered from copper mines and salt mines; textiles, leather, bone and wooden objects. It seems unlikely that this is due merely to the unfavourable physical conditions for decomposition; it is more likely that high concentrations of salt or of metal ions may inhibit bacterial and fungal decay.

AGRICULTURE

In Chapter 6 we shall deal with agriculture from the biological standpoint, but here mention must be made of those tools of the trade which turn up from time to time. Wooden implements not infrequently emerge from peat bogs; it was not always carelessness which put them there, for there is good evidence that sacrifices were made by bequeathing everyday articles of all sorts – even sometimes one's chieftain – to the insatiable maw of the bog. It is from such finds that we can learn how adzes and axes were hafted, and what woods were used. Hazel or ash were most usual, both flexible woods which do not easily split. A surprising exception was the axe from Ehenside Tarn[31] which was said to be hafted in beech. This seems an unsuitable choice of species, until we realize that this haft was in fact made out of a root.

Another agricultural object of which several examples – dating back to the Neolithic – are known is the yoke. It was used for yoking draft oxen and horses in teams drawing ploughs or wagons, as can be seen on many rock engravings. The yoke is among the many agricultural objects recovered from the waterlogged deposits of the Swiss pile-dwellings

(Tschumi, 1949). They also yielded various forms of sickle and reaping knife, some with the cutting flints still in position, and a long flexible threshing stick.

The plough is the most important agricultural implement and a good deal is known from prehistoric and later drawings about its development through the ages. It is not the sort of object which would find its way accidentally into a peat bog and would be of little use on swampy ground, so it is not surprising that we have few direct remains. Nevertheless, the almost complete spade-ard found at Døstrup in Jutland is a notable exception, and a number of others in a more or less fragmentary state enable us to build up a fairly complete picture.[30] Steensberg[153] has recently described and illustrated various wooden implements of cultivation, including the spade-like traction-ard which was pulled through the soil to make a furrow. It is very early in date, apparently ascribable to the transition from the Ertebølle to the Neolithic in Schleswig.

5

Plants used in ritual and medicine

Inevitably our knowledge of the uses of plants in this context must be fragmentary. We usually need the help of written history to enable us to interpret religious and superstitious beliefs, because the principles of these have not generally been passed down to us – or if they have they are too modified to be of any use. Most archaeologists at one time or another have taken refuge in the word 'ritual' to describe something which is inexplicable in the modern idiom; very often things obviously do have a ritual significance, but there are times when they seem to have no significance at all. In medical matters, too, modern attitudes are so vastly different from the primitive that interpretation is difficult, though in this case the lack of any direct evidence to go on is almost total.

A great deal can be learnt from studies of modern primitive people, and a great deal has been written on their beliefs and practices. These are so diverse, however, that rarely can one extrapolate from the present to the past with any certainty. Yarnell (1964) has recorded the many plants used for medicinal purposes or as charms by the North American Indians, but even among the different tribes there is a great diversity of practice. Such investigations merely make us alert to the possibility that many plants may be used in this way and that we may therefore come across their remains from time to time. By far the greatest number of plants recorded by Yarnell was used for making medicinal brews and beverages, and it is most unlikely that any recognizable trace of these would be recovered by archaeologists. However, it has already been pointed out that these brews probably supplied essential vitamins. Occasionally the need for these can be demonstrated. Other brews were used as charms for success in hunting or fishing, or to give protection against unpleasantnesses such as snakes. Others were used in love potions and as aphrodisiacs. The use of plants for smoking in order to attract deer has already been referred to, and smoking is another method of using plants for charm purposes. Smoking is an old custom in various parts of the world, and certainly dates back long before the discovery and use of tobacco, though the use of clay pipes for the purpose in West Africa does seem to be a direct copy of European practice. In North America stone and pottery pipes were used, but these were probably later than those of wood or cane. In the New World tobacco was the main material for smoking, sometimes adulterated with leaves of sumac (*Rhus* spp.) and the inner bark of dogwood (*Cornus* spp.), but in the Northwest it was used for chewing – mixed with shell lime – rather than for smoking, whilst in South America it was preferred as snuff (Driver, 1964).

The evidence of ritual practices which archaeology reveals nearly always relates to death and burial and rarely does it tell us anything about the ritual of life. However, we learn a good deal not only about the materials used in funerary ritual, but incidentally about normal day-to-day usage. For instance, Helbaek's study[71] of the remains of funeral meals in pre-urban Rome tells us not only what was being eaten at this rite but also sheds light on the methods by which meals were prepared and the foods used. Similarly, the Ancient Egyptian tombs have told us a great deal, as must already have been made apparent, about the contemporary technological attainments and practices.

The exceptional conditions of dryness have preserved for us in the Egyptian tombs a great deal of information about ritual practices and the materials used. Apart altogether from the remarkably successful practice of mummification itself, evidence has been forthcoming about the use of incense, oils and perfume, mostly of plant origin (Lucas, 1962). Incenses were prepared from gum-resins and true resins, the aromatic secretions of certain trees and shrubs. Frankincense was obtained from various species of *Boswellia*, small trees which grow in Arabia and Somaliland, and also from a Sudanese species, *Commiphora pedunculata*. Myrrh was also found in the tombs over a long span of time; it comes from other species of *Commiphora*, which also grow in Arabia and Somaliland. A number of other incenses, and resins of one form or another, have been found in the tombs. Occasionally, too, remains of small sticks of wood have been found in small vessels in the tombs; these were probably pieces of aromatic wood. Their actual identity is not known, but woods which could be used in this way occur in Kenya and Uganda.

From the tombs it has been deduced that use was also made of perfumes. These occurred as extracts in an oil or fat base. Whereas today plant perfumes are usually extracted in alcohol, this was not possible in Ancient Egypt since the distillation of alcohol had not yet been invented. Consequently the flowers, seeds, leaves, or whatever the odoriferous material, were steeped in oils or fats, in which the aromatic essences are soluble. The resulting unguents were used for anointing the body and were probably in general use in this hot, dry climate as skin and hair dressings. The fats used for this purpose were animal fats, and one can imagine that perfume was a desirable additive not only to camouflage any inherent aroma they may have, but also any that might develop. A number of vegetable oils were used: balanos oil, from the fruits of *Balanites aegyptica*, a tree once abundant in Egypt, but now rare; ben oil, from several species of *Moringa*; almond oil – a rarity, since almonds had to be imported; and castor oil, which was used, unperfumed, by the poor. Cedar oil was an important material in the preparation of the mummies; it did not come from cedar but from a juniper, just as the modern cedarwood oil comes in fact from an American species, *Juniperus virginiana*. Many other aromatic and preservative substances have been identified from the Egyptian tombs; indeed one wonders whether mummification could have been invented in any country lacking the botanical endowments of north-east Africa.

Outside the dry areas the available evidence of the use of plants is much less complete, though what we have may indicate the use of timber on a considerable scale. Perhaps the wooden henge monuments such as Woodhenge are most impressive in this respect. If Mrs Cunnington's reconstruction[28] is basically correct, such a monument would have contained a forest of straight timbers ranging up to 10 m in length. From the remains it was established that most of these were oak, though birch and even pine were also represented. The occurrence of pine at this time (Bronze Age) is noteworthy, since this species had very largely disappeared from southern England, except perhaps for swampy and coastal sites, some 2,000 years earlier. I, too, have identified pine from the Bronze Age, from the mass of charcoal in a ritual pit under a barrow at Chick's Hill in Dorset,[6] so it may be that pine had some significance of which we now know nothing. Timber works are frequently recognized – or at least their remains are – in burial structures: palisades of various degrees of impressiveness, mortuary houses, and in exceptional cases elaborate wagon-burials. In some tumuli coffins have been found, hewn out of a single piece of oak or occasionally elm, and in many other cases traces of what might have been a coffin are found as little more than humic stains in the earth. How this contrasts with the preservation of papyrus-built coffins from the Ancient Egyptian tombs! Yet even in Egypt massive timber must have been used; we have already mentioned the use of timber rollers to move the blocks of which the pyramids were built, and we can only guess at the heavyweight apparatus which would be needed to place these blocks in position. By these standards the erection of the trilithons at Stonehenge is small beer, yet even this operation would have required a massive staging and leverage system of heavy timbers.

A particularly interesting find is reported by Neustupny[115] in a neolithic context in southern Moravia. A jug-like vessel of modified Baalbergia type was found to contain leaves of *Allium*, probably a wild species, from which the tips and bases had been cut. Neustupny traces the uses of this genus (onions, leeks and garlic) for food, medicine and magic from earliest times to the present.

Intoxication by one means or another is a feature of many ritual practices today and doubtless this was so in ancient times too. The intoxicant effect of alcohol must have been known as long as fermented liquors have been known, and that in turn is probably just as long as man has been making starchy gruels and sugary beverages. It has been seriously argued, though not generally agreed, that cereal cultivation arose in order to provide beer in the first place, and farinaceous food only secondarily.[12] However that may be, it can be assumed that fermented drinks were made long before agriculture came in, and apart from their alimentary properties they were no doubt used to produce intoxication. Spirits, as we have said, were a late development, certainly not earlier than classical times, and possibly as late as the Middle Ages.

Intoxication can also be brought about by other means. Certain fungi can produce a form of intoxication accompanied by hallucinations; for instance the fly agaric (*Amanita muscoides*) is used to produce these effects by some peoples of Kamchatka. There is also a tradition of uncertain antiquity that the Vikings deliberately used it in order to go berserk. However deeply the results are ingrained in the minds of men, such uses leave no trace that the archaeologist can pick up. An understanding of plant ecology may enable us to predict that such a species would have been present and if it were it is reasonable to assume that its properties would be known. The same is no doubt true of narcotics; but in this case the plants were brought into cultivation. The opium poppy (*Papaver somniferum*) has been cultivated since neolithic times, perhaps in the first place for poppy-seed oil, but who can doubt that its narcotic property enhanced its value. Hemp (*Cannabis sativa*) has a similar history; it is valuable not only for fibre and oil-seed, but as a source of hashish or marijuana. Although a plant of warmer climates, it does grow under British conditions, and indeed was a compulsory crop in Tudor times. That it should be necessary to enforce the growing of hemp by law may seem surprising, until one realizes that in the British climate the plant only produces significant amounts of the narcotic alkaloid in exceptionally hot and dry summers.

As already said, direct evidence of the medical uses of plants is very slight. Nevertheless, we can infer some of the uses. In discussing the diet of primitive man we referred several times to the value of plants and the foods and beverages made from them as sources of vitamins or trace elements. The North American Indian may not have known, for instance, that Saskatoon berries contain three times as much copper and iron as prunes or raisins, but they doubtless recognized that they had some beneficial effect. In other cases there can be no doubt that the special properties of certain plants were well known; coca, quinine and curare were all introduced to us through the natives of South America.

The condition of skeletons can sometimes indicate significant aspects of life and diet. Up till the Neolithic, advanced decay of teeth was not a characteristic of primitive man, but in some places it is unusually marked. It was so, for instance, among the Californian Indians, and this has been attributed to their habit of leaching the tannins out of the acorns, which were their staple food, through a bed of sand. The meal thereby became contaminated with sand and caused excessive erosion of the teeth. When one considers the amount of wear on quern stones, this could have been a factor in agricultural communities also. Deformation of bone structure is sometimes apparent in skeletons;[172] this can be due to malnutrition or to food deficiencies associated with malnutrition. The concentration on one or two starchy products to the exclusion of vitamin-rich foods led to diseases such as rickets and scurvy, whose ravages left traces in the skeletons. Beri-beri, the scourge of rice-eating people, known in China in the 3rd century B.C., was not only serious on its own account, but was often associated with general lowering of resistance to infection. Chronic malnutrition in childhood was commonplace and early death usual. Where dependence was on one crop a bad harvest could spell disaster and this was not entirely a matter of weather. Disease could strike the crop. Rust spores have been found in an archaeological context,[5] and ergot was another pest of wheat and rye, not only reducing the yield but rendering the flour poisonous. Perhaps we too readily assume that the introduction of agriculture took the hazards out of life. It may not always have turned out that way; by fostering too great a dependence on one crop deficiency diseases could be encouraged, and the hazards of a bad harvest rendered extremely severe.

6

Cultivated plants

So far we have been tracing as well as we can the ways in which the wild plant environment supported man's needs in the days before he had developed alternative sources through metallurgy and through cultivation. Today we may realize that we are still largely dependent upon plant and animal foods, but it is not so obvious that practically all these are grown by man specifically for his own purposes. Even our timber supply is derived more and more from cultivated crops as the wild species of the forest are systematically worked out. Especially do we fail to realize, unless we are widely read or travelled, that the cultivated species we are familiar with are only a small proportion of all the plants which are grown by man in the various regions of the earth. Add to this the oft-quoted statement that no major crop has been brought into cultivation from the wild during the past 5,000 years, and we see at once the enormous importance of what prehistoric man achieved. This is simply but dramatically expressed in another way. It has been calculated that if man had never progressed beyond the hunting and food-gathering stage, the maximum population which the world's surface could support any one time would be 20–30 million people. The present population is of the order of 4,000 million; the difference between the two has been made possible by cultivation. And some geographers are sanguine that modern techniques make it theoretically possible to feed several times that number. However, this controversial issue is fortunately not within our present terms of reference, so we can turn back to the early stages of the process without worrying our heads about how, when, or whether ultimate disaster will come.

Life at simple subsistence level probably did not allow much time for admiring the scenery and thinking deep thoughts, whilst in the higher latitudes it must have been distinctly uncomfortable during the winter season. Nevertheless, as we have seen, even there the environment provided for men's needs in food and shelter, and nearer the tropics conditions would be correspondingly less difficult. This adequacy of supply is an important point, for it has often been assumed that man was driven to 'invent' cultivation because as his numbers increased and, some say, as the climate became drier, he was not able to exist above starvation level by hunting and gathering. This point of view has generally been expressed by those whose main preoccupation is the rise of cereal agriculture in the Near East. If, however, we take a broader view, this conclusion is not so convincing.

In the first place, it is not certain that the domestication of cereal grasses was the earliest form of cultivation. Sauer (1952) has argued very cogently that the simplest and most direct way of bringing a plant into cultivation is by transplanting it or at least a piece of it; that is, by vegetative propagation. In fact there are people living today who practise cultivation in this manner (vegeculture), but are unaware of the possibility of seed propagation – it is not obvious to them. The same mystery about reproduction by seed underlies Christ's words: 'Except a corn of wheat fall into the ground and die, it abideth alone; but if it die, it bringeth forth much fruit' (John xii. 24). Now if it is correct that vegetative cultivation was the earliest form, then it is likely that this took place in the wet tropics, where the high temperatures and abundant moisture are just those conditions which we try to create in our own hothouses when we wish to propagate plants vegetatively. Indeed, vegeculture is a strong feature of tropical agriculture even today. However, if these were the conditions under which the earliest farming took place, then it is unlikely that it happened through necessity in a region where plant growth is so abundant. Indeed, it may be that the earliest cultigens were not food plants but useful or ornamental plants. A study of animal domestication leads to a similar conclusion; the earliest animals domesticated seemed to have had ritual and prestige significance in the first place and only later were used for food. Some South American tribes have the domestic fowl, but they do not eat either it or its eggs.

Though it does not follow that the reasons which lay behind the development of farming in the wet tropics applied with the same force to more arid areas such as the Near East, nevertheless there is no good evidence that necessity was the mother of the invention of seed agriculture. This is borne out by many studies of hunter–gatherer communities today.[98] Sauer argues with pertinence that people who are on the verge of starvation are not likely to think out and experiment with a completely new and untried way of life. It would involve more than growing the food.

There would have to be a certain degree of settlement to protect and tend the crops, and this in itself would mean abandoning the way of life which they knew and understood. Perhaps there was already an increasing degree of settlement among the sheep-herders, though there would still have to be seasonal movement.

Archaeology has an important part to play in our understanding of the origins of agriculture because it is mostly on archaeological sites that crop remains are preserved; moreover, the archaeological setting can provide a date for the botanical evidence. The earliest records of agriculture are in the so-called Fertile Crescent of the Near East (Fig. 2), with dates

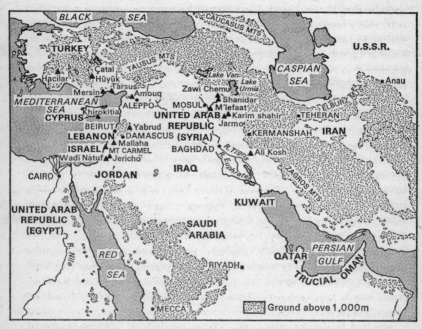

2. The Near East, showing sites where the earliest agriculture was taking place.

around 10,000 years ago, but the earliest dates for the New World and the Far East are also approaching that figure. The idea that agriculture arose once only and then spread throughout the world is no longer tenable. Sauer (1952) suggested that there were 'hearths' of domestication in various parts of the world, but there is no unanimity over the question of which 'hearths' were primary and which might be secondary. Harlan[64] has made the interesting suggestion that there were only three centres of agricultural origin, but that each was associated with a much wider area in which domestication was developed and many new species were brought in from the wild. The latter he called non-centres because of their great spread. The centres he would recognize are Meso-America, the Near East, and North China; their associated non-centres are South America, Central Africa, and South-East Asia with the South Pacific. He makes the interesting suggestion that what was being exchanged and developed between a centre and its non-centres was not so much the domesticated crops themselves as ideas about domestication.

We are still left with the question as to why agriculture arose in these centres at about the same time. It has been suggested that the spontaneous growth of seeds on middens and other deposits associated with man's occupation sites may have given him the idea of seed cultivation and pointed to plants that could be domesticated. This 'rubbish heap' hypothesis, however, fails to explain why the origins should have been roughly contemporaneous or why there should be so few centres. Moreover the crops which were domesticated are not always those which grow in such situations.[66] Other explanations have been sought in man's sociocultural development,[18] and this is perhaps one of the few explanations not open to the objection that the circumstances in which agriculture arose must have had their parallels many times before in human history. However, it still seems possible that some environmental change provided the motivation for man to exercise his inventiveness: what has been called the 'shock stimulus'.[152] An early hypothesis of this sort was put forward by Childe[26] who believed, on the incomplete evidence of his day, that in the Near East the change from the end of the Pleistocene to the beginning of the Post-glacial was marked by a climatic change from humid conditions to increased desiccation. This, he thought, would concentrate plants, animals and man himself in oases, and through propinquity this would lead to domestication. We now know that the climatic change at this time was from cold arid conditions to warmer conditions with more rainfall, particularly in the winter. The suggestion has been made by Wright[182] that it was not until this change had taken place that wild cereal grasses were able to reach the Near East in the developing Mediterranean climate and so became available for domestication, though Wright recognized that the question remains as to why domestication did not take place in the original refugia, such as North Africa. There may be other factors involved and recently Whyte[176, 177] has drawn attention to a change on the part of the plants themselves that may be a necessary precursor to domestication. He points out that cultivated cereals and grain legumes are annuals, though the wild ancestors are normally perennials. He believes that this change from the perennial to the annual habit may be brought about by fluctuations in environmental factors, and for East Asia he suggests that periods of domestication associated with great diurnal and seasonal variation in temperatures may have triggered the change. Perennials, he believes, would be at a disadvantage, whereas a plant which perennates by seed would survive. Interestingly, he takes the argument a stage further and suggests that overgrazing by early pastoralists/hunters/collectors may have contributed to desiccation and if this were so it may suggest an interaction between man and micro-climate which might have occurred in those regions of the world where a Mediterranean-type climate was becoming established at the beginning of the Post-glacial period.

It is beyond the scope of this book to deal with the rapidly growing body of knowledge about the origins of crops and the genetical and morphological changes brought about by domestication. Renfrew (1973) has dealt with the botany and archaeological context of the important food plants of the Old World, and symposium volumes edited by Ucko and Dimbleby (1969) and Struever[155] contain extensive papers dealing with ecological, genetical and cultural aspects of early agriculture. For the present purpose all that can be done is to outline the course of development of a few of the more important crop plants, particularly those which figured in the earliest centres of origin of agriculture.

Though seed agriculture embraces many families, it is the cereal grasses that have been most importantly associated with man's advancement; wheat and barley originated in the Near East, rice in South-East Asia and maize (corn) in Meso-America. In addition legumes have been important early domesticates in America and in eastern Asia.

Wheat (*Triticum*)

The history of the wheat is a complex one, upon which a great deal of genetical work has been done.[134, 187] There were two primary ancestors, wild einkorn (*T. boeoticum*) and wild emmer (*T. monococcoides*). Wild einkorn is a diploid ($2n = 14$) and it gives rise to a diploid cultivated einkorn (*T. monococcum*), still occasionally to be found as a crop. The cultivated and wild forms are interfertile and are no more than races of the same species. The only apparent difference between them is that the rachis (main stalk) of the ear is less brittle in the cultivated form, apparently the result of collecting and harvesting. This means that natural dispersal is restricted in the cultivated einkorn, so that survival depends on man.[187] In both types the grain is hulled; that is, the kernel remains ensheathed in the glumes. This primitive wheat became widely distributed and was the wheat of the first agriculture to reach Britain.

The wild emmer also gave rise to a cultivated form, *T. dicoccum*, and here too there is a parallel development of a tougher rachis, and the grains remain hulled. Emmer differs from einkorn in being a tetraploid ($2n = 28$), having apparently been derived by allopolyploidy from a cross between einkorn and a wild grass, probably *Aegilops speltoides*. Packets of genetical material, referred to as genomes, can be recognized as having come from einkorn (genome A) and from *Aegilops* (genome B). There is a range of tetraploids with this AB make-up; for details see Peterson.[122] Cultivated emmer became the most widely distributed wheat of antiquity, being known from the 8th millennium B.C. in Iran. It occurred in pre-dynastic sites in Egypt and is found in the early civilizations of Mesopotamia, India and Ethiopia. It spread westwards probably along the Mediterranean and also with the Danubians, reaching Britain and Scandinavia. It did not take over from einkorn immediately on arrival, but after a period of consolidation it was general throughout the late Neolithic.

The third wheat we must briefly consider is bread wheat (*T. aestivum*). This is a hexaploid wheat ($2n = 42$), originating as an allopolyploid from a natural crossing between an AB wheat of the emmer group (opinions differ as to which one) and another wild grass *Aegilops squarrosa* (genome D). Wheats of this type are the ancestors of our modern bread wheats. This genetical development conferred several useful characters on this type: the grain contains gluten, which means that the dough can be leavened: the grain is now naked, falling free of the chaff and so simplifying threshing; and perhaps most important, the environmental adaptability of this wheat has made it possible to develop forms suitable for a wide range of climatic conditions, a character perhaps derived from the wild grass, which has a very wide range in Europe and Asia. It is still not known how and when the out-crossing took place which produced this cultivar, which is known from the 6th millennium B.C. in Iran and Anatolia. It may have arisen as a weed in emmer fields in the first instance before being selected for its own sake. It eventually spread widely and reached Britain in the Iron Age. Though the ABD genetic make-up of this wheat is firmly established, experimental attempts to reconstitute it from its putative parents have produced not bread wheat but spelt (*T. spelta*). Spelt is a hexaploid, but has some primitive characters such as hulled grain. It is surprising that its occurrence in the archaeological record is very much later than bread wheat, so that it cannot be regarded as ancestral to bread wheat.

BARLEY (*Hordeum*)

Together with the wheats, the barleys form the earliest cereals known to man: there are records from Iran and Anatolia at about 7000 B.C. Though there are several varieties of barley, the evolutionary history of the cultivated barleys is less complex than that of the wheats. The structure of the ear can vary considerably in appearance in the different barleys, some having two clearly opposed rows of grains, others having six rows. This is not such a fundamental difference as it might sound. Each spikelet contains one central floret and two lateral ones, which in the 2-row barleys are abortive and therefore do not contribute to the ear. A minor genetic change will render these lateral florets fertile, so that three grains are produced from each spikelet, giving the 6-row structure to the ear.

It has been argued that the 2- and 6-row forms are derived from different ancestors, but attempts to find a separate wild 6-row form have proved fruitless, and one is not known from the archaeological record. The view is now generally held that there is only one ancestor for all the cultivated barleys, namely *H. spontaneum*, the wild 2-row barley. This has turned up in sites of the 7th and 8th millennium B.C. in the Fertile Crescent. As in the wheats, one of the first changes brought about by domestication is the increased toughness of the rachis. Beyond this, a sequence of development is difficult to establish. There is no known history of outcrossing in the barleys, and there is no polyploidy; all are diploids ($2n = 14$). However, among the cultivars there are both 2- and 6-row barleys and within each there are both naked- and hulled-grained forms.

Barley was an important crop throughout the prehistoric period of agriculture and has spread throughout the Old World, extending from remote parts of Britain (Orkneys) in the West, to China in the East. At times it superseded wheat as the main crop, at least until bread wheats arrived. In Britain it was the most abundant grain from the Neolithic to the Viking period. Today, it still forms as much as 40% of the grain we grow, but it is now used mainly for animal feed or brewing.

OATS (*Avena*) AND RYE (*Secale*)

Both these cereals are important today, particularly on poorer soils or under climatic conditions less favourable for wheat or barley. Both cereals have been derived from weed grasses, and appear relatively late in the archaeological record. There are several cultivated oats, showing varying degrees of polyploidy, and perhaps derived from different wild ancestors. Their history is rendered difficult to unravel by the fact that cultivated types have reverted to the wild, perhaps more than once. Oats appeared in Britain in the Iron Age, where it was sporadic, but at some Roman sites in Scotland it appears to have been the main cereal.

The wild ancestor of rye is not known for certain, but may be *S. montanum*. This species is a perennial, but the cultivar is annual. Rye is more tolerant of difficult climatic conditions than wheat, and therefore tended to replace wheat in fields at higher altitudes or latitudes. A climatic deterioration at the beginning of the Iron Age in Europe favoured rye along the northern and western fringes of agriculture. It began to appear in British sites in the Iron Age, perhaps first as a weed, but by medieval times it was a staple cereal and is still to be seen on the poorer and drier soils in eastern England. Rye is wind-pollinated and therefore its presence may be reflected in pollen spectra.

MAIZE (*Zea mays*)

The interest in the origins of maize by plant geneticists has led to intensive field investigations to establish its ancestry and where it arose. It is widely believed that there is no known ancestor of this cereal in existence today. The archaeological benefits of this enquiry have been profound; the known history of agriculture in the New World has been more than doubled as a result.

This line of research was chiefly instigated by the Harvard geneticist Professor Paul Mangelsdorf. His recent book, *Corn*,[105] brings together the evidence he has collected, with full accounts of the archaeological material which has been discovered. Like wheat, maize has undergone a long morphological and genetical development, including hybridization with a wild grass *Tripsacum*, a related species. As a result of breeding together primitive forms of maize, Mangelsdorf produced a plant with very different characteristics from the maize we know. The male and female inflorescences were on the same spike, not separated spatially on the plant as in modern forms. The enclosing husk, which in modern forms prevents seed dispersal, did not enclose the cob completely, and the cobs were only a few centimetres long.

From his breeding work Mangelsdorf produced a model of what he believed the primitive maize cob would have looked like, and interdisciplinary archaeological expeditions under the direction of Richard Mac-Neish were organized to search for such primitive cobs. In dry caves in the Tehuacán valley in Mexico small cobs of a primitive type, about 5 cm in length, were found dating back to the 6th millennium B.C. and these were claimed by Mangelsdorf as wild maize. We cannot list his reasons here, but they did not convince all plant geneticists. In particular, Professor George Beadle[15] has other views: he does not accept that no wild ancestor exists; he believes that it is with us all the time in the form of teosinte (*Zea mexicana*), a plant with a long history of cultivation in its own right. In fact it has been found in an archaeological context dated to 5600 B.C. or more. The scientific argument is not resolved yet, but the archaeological implications are enthralling.

Before leaving the cereals and turning to the protein-rich legumes, it is appropriate to discuss briefly the protein content of the cereals themselves. In contrast to vegetative storage organs such as roots, cereal grains contain a proportion of protein in addition to the starch bulk. This means that as a food they are better balanced, though in modern cereals there is a deficiency of amino-acids such as tryptophane and lysine, which are essential to health. Modern wheats have about 10-12% protein, but primitive wheats grown on an experimental Iron Age farm at Butser Hill in Southern England have been found to have much higher quantities: 19% of protein has been determined in emmer wheat. The wild *Triticum boeoticum* has a higher content even than this, and it seems that there is a wider range of amino-acids. The implications of this in relation to food-collecting are important, and it is equally interesting to realize that the increased production of modern cereals seems to have been achieved largely through the addition of carbohydrate.

In all primitive agricultural systems leguminous crops have appeared early on the scene; doubtless their value as protein foods were recognized, if not in those terms. In the Near East peas, lentils and vetches are found in the early deposits; in the earliest ones it may be wild pulses that are present – size is the main criterion of domestication – but larger-sized seeds in later deposits suggest domestication. The horse-bean *Vicia faba*, a forerunner of our broad bean, was cultivated relatively late though its wild ancestor was present at Beidhe at about 7000 B.C. Whyte[177] has discussed the origin of the food legumes in Asia, but dating evidence is not yet as complete here as it is in Meso-America.

Phaseolus

The genus *Phaseolus* has been the subject of research by geneticists and others concerned with crop evolution.[148] The genetical work is beyond our scope in this book, but the archaeological history of these beans, which include runner and kidney beans, is remarkable. Four species have been studied in detail, viz. *Ph. lunatus, Ph. coccineus, Ph. acutifolius* and *Ph. vulgaris*. At Tehuacán in Mexico *Ph. vulgaris* was recorded at 5600 B.C., *Ph. acutifolius* at 3500 B.C. and *Ph. coccineus* at about 250 B.C. The last-named, however, has a possible date of more than 6000 B.C. at Ocampo in Mexico. *Ph. lunatus* is recorded at 4000 B.C. at Chilce in Peru, and there is botanical evidence that this species was domesticated independently in Peru and Mexico. The early pods and beans of *Ph. vulgaris* are quite comparable in size to modern beans, suggesting that domestication produced rapid changes. *Ph. acutifolius* is an annual plant, but the other three show the transition from perennial to annual tendencies which Whyte[177] noted for the Asian beans. These pulses contain the amino-acids lysine and tryptophane which are deficient in maize, the staple cereal of the New World.

Whilst dealing with the New World, mention should be made of two other genera which, together with *Phaseolus*, were some of the earliest cultivars in this continent, namely the cucurbits (squashes, gourds, melons, etc.) and the chili peppers (*Capsicum*). These and a number of other food plants have been identified from dry-cave deposits in Mexico; a rich source of remains of these food plants are the coprolites which are well preserved in such conditions (see pp. 95–6).

CUCURBITS (see also p. 84)

The seeds of cucurbits are found in coprolites in dry-cave deposits, but in the deposits themselves the shells of the fruits and the peduncles of the fruits may be found, together with seeds, in considerable quantity. Using such material, from which identification of the cultivars is possible (though the wild species pose problems), Whitaker and his colleagues have been able to build up a record of these plants through archaeological sequences in Mexico[175] and Peru. In the Ocampo caves the earliest levels (Infiernielo culture, over 6000 B.C.) seeds of the cultivated *Cucurbita pepo* (pumpkin and squash), occurring together with seeds of wild species, represent the earliest record in Meso-America, and pre-date the appearance of maize by 1,000 years. Other cultivated species of *Cucurbita* appear later in the prehistoric sequences.

The gourd, *Lagenaria siceraria*, is also found at the earliest levels at Ocampo. This is an Old World species, morphologically very variable, but the characters of the seeds suggest that it came over from Africa, probably by oceanic drift.

CHILI PEPPERS (*Capsicum*)

The remains of the fruits of peppers have been identified in early sites in Mexico and Peru.[124] There are several species, some of which have both wild and cultivated forms. The effect of cultivation has been to produce an enormous range of size, colour and shape in the fruits. The earliest records are in pre-agricultural contexts in Mexico, but Callen[22] recognized *Capsicum* remains in coprolites in the levels of the Ocampo culture in caves near Tamaulipas, that is in levels where the cultivated cucurbits were also turning up. Certainly cultivated peppers were being grown in coastal Peru by 2000 B.C. The peppers illustrate the different directions which early agriculture took in Mexico and in South America, reminding us of Harlan's distinction between centres and non-centres of agricultural origins.[64]

There is not space even to survey the many species which have been cultivated in systems of vegeculture, so we will leave this sketch of the cultivated food plants with a brief mention of just one ancient and important crop, the yam.

Yams (*Dioscorea* spp.)[3, 4]

There are three main geographical groups of yams: Asiatic, African and American. Their genetical characters are complex; multiple polyploidy reflects the complexity of their development, and this probably reflects a long history of propagation vegetatively rather than by seed. The chromosome numbers of the Old World yams are mostly in multiples of 10, whilst the New World ones are based on the number 9. This probably reflects a long genetical isolation. Indeed, the American yams are of little cultural significance and will not be discussed further. Today the yams grown in the New World are nearly all species of Old World origin.

A number of different species are grown in the geographical groups; for a more detailed account reference should be made to the paper by Alexander and Coursey.[4] The yams exemplify the three non-centres listed by Harlan,[64] and there seems no doubt that domestication has taken place independently in each area. In some cases the wild progenitors are not known. Some species, e.g. *D. hispida* and some wild species, contain a highly toxic alkaloid which has to be removed, yet one more example of food plants with a poisonous element (see Chapter 2).

Yams are climbing plants producing underground tubers which form the food source in this crop. Species vary in the size and number of tubers they produce, but some can be enormous, specimens weighing as much as 50 kg having been recorded, though 5–10 kg is more usual. The food material is starch, with a very low protein content. As yams grow in tropical areas and have no hard parts the chances of finding actual plant material are remote. Our evidence for yam cultivation in the past has to be indirect, based on cultivation tools and, where possible, the micro-contours of the fields. Yams are frequently grown on mounds which could leave traces if an old land surface becomes buried.

On the basis of cultural and indirect evidence such as that just mentioned, it seems likely that yams were being cultivated in Eastern India by the late 3rd–2nd millennium B.C., as early as any other known crop in that region. There is evidence of the spread of cultivated yams from Asia to Africa. *D. alata* is found in South-East Asia, where it probably originated, and also in West Africa. Tentative evidence suggests that it became established there in the 1st millennium B.C. Much more evidence needs to be accumulated before we can gauge the age of yam cultivation, but on soci-cultural as well as technological grounds it appears to be a crop of very respectable antiquity.

Some mention must be made of plants cultivated for their usefulness rather than for food. Plants were grown for their fibres (hemp, flax); for dyes (woad, saffron); for constructional purposes (palms, reeds and, later, forest trees). The gourd is a very special case; it had been cultivated in both Old and New Worlds even before Columbus, and though there is only one species, *Lagenaria siceraria*, its varieties are endless, as are the shapes and therefore the uses of its fruits.

Perhaps flax (*Linum*) has played the greatest part as a fibre plant in Old World prehistory. Moreover flax is important as an oil-seed (linseed), another important category of cultigen we have had to leave out of consideration. Indeed, the cultivation of flax was probably a double event, determined by climate.[73] The wild species, *L. bienne*, has two races, one which is more or less perennial, growing in the coastal belts of Atlantic Europe and the Mediterranean, the other being a winter annual, growing in the foothills bordering the Euphrates–Tigris plain – in fact the cradle of agriculture again. Cultivated flax (*L. usitatissimum*) is a very varied plant with a range from Western Europe to Western Asia. In some places, for example in Iraq, it is grown as a winter annual for oil production, the seeds being harvested in early summer. In Egypt, on the other hand, a summer annual form is grown for fibre, not for seed. In view of the different behaviour of the wild races it seems likely that these two forms of use have been developed independently. However, there are many details yet to be filled in and these must come largely from archaeological sites, particularly from preserved grains or grain impressions, whose size and shape is what the botanist wants to know. The earliest known record of cultivated flax is in the 7th millennium B.C.[185] and the plant is still cultivated today. Archaeologists specializing in almost any phase of the Post-glacial may therefore have some contribution to make to this important and intriguing study.

Gold of Pleasure (*Camelina sativa*), also known as false flax, was often associated with flax, probably occurring as a weed in flax fields. It was cultivated in its own right as an oil crop as far back as the Neolithic, and so has continued on the Continent until quite recent times, though it is now almost extinct as a cultivated plant and relatively rare even as a weed. It is a member of the Cruciferae, the cress family, a family abounding in useful plants and troublesome weeds. Recently it has been found that *Camelina* has an apparent toxic effect on flax; even a few plants contaminating a flax field can significantly reduce the yield. Archaeologists would no doubt attribute changes in the relative importance of *Camelina* and *Linum* to cultural factors, but they could be quite wrong.

Another point on which archaeology might have something to say is the rather odd fact that quite a number of our cultivated plants were derived – long ago – from plants of the sea coast. Cabbage (*Brassica*), with all its many variants, is probably the oldest example, but others are beet (*Beta vulgaris*), fennel (*Foeniculum vulgare*), seakale (*Crambe maritima*) and asparagus (*A. officinalis*). Probably the list can be extended. All these have been cultivated in the first place as leaf-vegetables and identifiable remains in archaeological sites are unlikely to be met but they may point to a certain importance of the coastal habitat; it seems likely that the Mediterranean was the main centre of domestication of this group of plants.

Finally, a brief mention must be made of the weeds of cultivation, a big subject in its own right. Cultivated land is land where the natural competition, for instance by trees, is eliminated or at least reduced, and this allows plants to grow which would otherwise be ousted. We now know that some of the weeds of our fields were abundant at the beginning of the Post-glacial period, before the forest had invaded the grassland and parkland. Once the trees attained dominance these plants became rare, only to come into their own again when man opened up the forest. Others doubtless came in from the Continent by normal migration, but there must also have been many which were assisted, consciously or unconsciously, by man. Until recent times the carrying of crop seed has been a prolific source of new weeds, many of which do not survive in the new habitat, but others do. Recent genetic research is showing that many of our weeds are polyploids, particularly those which proliferate vegetatively – by runners, bulbils, suckers, and so on – rather than by seed. Some familiar examples are couch-grass (*Agropyron repens*), stinging nettle and white clover (*Trifolium repens*). It may be that man has provided the conditions for polyploidy to arise very much as he seems to have done with the cultigens. These polyploids may in fact be developed from wild ancestors which had a more restricted ecological habitat, but as the result of genetic development they have acquired a cosmopolitan taste. Certainly the weeds of the Old World may be found in all parts of the world where the climate is not too extreme, and many of them may have acquired this aggressive power back in prehistoric times. There is not space to say more here; those who would like to know more about the biological and human relationships of weeds will find Sir Edward Salisbury's *Weeds and Aliens* (1964) a book of absorbing interest.

Part 2

The nature of the evidence

7

The preservation of plant material

The plant body is composed of materials performing two main functions: mechanical or skeletal, and life and growth. Plants differ from animals in that their cells have walls, and the walls are the source of their rigidity. They became modified to produce tissue with mechanical strength and clearly the ways in which this can be done are potentially far more varied than in animals, which generally have either an endoskeleton (e.g. vertebrates such as ourselves) or an exoskeleton (e.g. a lobster). In plants strengthening tissue can be laid down in almost any part of the plant. The vital material is contained within the cells, though in some tissues, such as wood, the cells have become converted to a purely mechanical function. Wood vessels and fibres lose their living contents once they have reached their full size and the strengthening materials have been laid down; they are dead tissues (though as will be seen in Chapter 8 they may be intimately associated with other living tissues).

Taking the green flowering plant as our model, its form is largely determined in broad outline by what it must do to feed itself and reproduce itself. Sunlight is the energy source for the conversion of carbon dioxide and water into carbohydrates (photosynthesis). There must be organs (usually leaves, but not always) which can trap the sunlight, there must be special conducting tissue which can take the products of photosynthesis away from the leaves to the other parts of the plant for use or for storage. At the same time all the living cells need oxygen for respiration and must get rid of the resultant carbon dioxide – some of which in daylight can be used for photosynthesis. It may be necessary for special tissues to be formed to effect this gas exchange, for example the spongy tissue (aerenchyma) of the roots and rhizomes of aquatic plants. Then the plant must be anchored in one place and its roots at the same time serve to provide it with water and nutrients from the soil. Finally, it must reproduce itself by flower and fruit.

There is no firm guide as to the parts of plants which the archaeologist may come across. There will inevitably be the accidental inclusion of plant remains with little or no practical significance, but man will often leave behind traces of those plants he was using. In the first part of this book we have seen over and over again that almost every conceivable part of many plants may be of use to man: bark, stem, roots, leaves, flowers, fruit, fibres and so on. The mechanical tissues of the plant serve man's mechanical needs, the storage tissues serve him as food, and doubtless the showy part, the flower, served him as ornament. We may therefore expect almost any type of tissue to have been left in an occupation site. How do these tissues vary in their powers of resisting decay?

To answer this it is necessary to say a little about the agents of decay or decomposition. In the wild state, as for instance in the forest, dead plant material is immediately subject to three processes. The first of these is simply comminution – the reducing of the plant part, whatever it is, to particles of smaller dimension. This process, in fact, may already have been responsible for the death of the material: the cow ingests living grass leaves, but when it has finished with them they are dead and broken up. Dead material, however, is the staple food of many soil animals[169] – earthworms, millipedes, springtails, mites, etc. – and each does a share of comminution until the fragments are of microscopic size. This process serves to make it easier for the second process, namely digestion, to operate. In digestion soluble nutrients are dissolved out of the dead tissue and absorbed by the feeding organism; the digestive juices contain chemicals and enzymes which render the plant material more soluble; protein, for instance, will be hydrolysed to absorbable amino-acids. Digestion may go on either internally, as with the animals already mentioned which actually ingest their food; or externally, as with organisms such as fungi and bacteria which live on the dead tissue. In fact, these can both go on at the same time; herbivorous animals rely on the intestinal flora of cellulose-converting bacteria to produce soluble sugars from insoluble cellulose. Ultimately comminution and digestion will reduce the plant material to simple inorganic substances. The third process referred to is the loss of soluble substances which is always liable to occur when the plant tissue is lying on or in the ground – the leaching out of breakdown products of the various stages of decay by organisms.

Plant materials vary a great deal in their resistance to decay; and different environments can promote different types of decomposition. Clearly the soluble parts of the living cell go first, quickly followed by those materials which can be transformed into solubles, e.g. starch, protein. The cell walls are more resistant. All walls are basically of cellulose, but other substances may be laid down on top of the cellulose in tissues having special functions. The epidermal cells may be coated with cutin to reduce water loss; cork cells become suberized, also waterproofing; wood cells become lignified, lignin being deposited to give strength. These different substances have different resistances to decay. So we find the beautiful leaf skeletons left behind in the spring, when the more readily destructible cellulose tissues – the soft parts of the leaf – have been destroyed quicker than the more resistant lignified ribs and veins. Later even the lignin goes, leaving no trace recognizable to the naked eye. On some soils, however, the lignin goes before the cellulose. Recent work has shown this to be true of heath soils and certain types of acid woodland soils (raw humus);[63] the cellulose is 'protected' by a resistant deposit and may persist for many years. The most resistant organic materials in the plant world are the walls of some pollen grains and especially fern spores; these will be discussed in greater detail in Chapter 9.

It is not beyond the bounds of possibility that one day the biochemist will enable us to deduce the previous presence of plant material even though all visible trace has gone. At the moment, however, we cannot do this with any degree of specificity, so we are dependent on visually recognizable residues. In other words, we can only identify plant material from the past if the processes described above have been arrested or inhibited so that the form of the structures still remains. The comminution of plant remains is the most serious form of decomposition, though as we shall see later, even microscopic fragments can sometimes tell us something. Moreover, a piece of wood, for example, may be partly decayed by fungi and still be recognizable as long as it is not fragmented. There does come the point, however, where fungal decay has gone so far that the tissues are completely disorganized and recognition is no longer possible. In archaeological sites the plant remains, as we have seen, are mainly of things used by man or stored for consumption; they are not in general comminuted. Whether they become comminuted later, by soil fauna, depends on the nature of the site. In the tropics termites soon seek out plant remains and leave practically no trace. In temperate regions the soil animals are less voracious, and they are frequently excluded by the activities on the site. If the site is indoors, for instance, it will become too dry for them, especially if there are hearths giving artificial heat. Heavy trampling of the ground also acts against them by reducing the porosity and therefore the aeration of the soil. The great majority of such animals needs an oxygen-rich atmosphere in which to live.

The same is generally true of the micro-organisms which decay plant materials, particularly fungi and bacteria (including actinomyces); the species important in these processes of decay are for the most part aerobic. There are other features of the micro-environment, too, that are important if these organisms are to be able to function. There must be adequate moisture present. Bacteria are unicellular organisms and so are closely dependent on their immediate surroundings. Water is the basis of all life, and if it is in short supply either it must be obtained from elsewhere (e.g. by a deep root-system), which bacteria cannot do, or growth – and perhaps even life – must stop. Temperature is another factor which has a direct effect on living tissues, including the decay organisms; the prevention of decay by refrigeration is a household notion today. High temperatures, too, can be inimical to life, but in the hot climates of the earth, it is usually excessive dryness rather than high temperature which prevents decay. Decay can be very rapid in the hot, humid tropics. Many bacteria are sensitive to their chemical surroundings, such as the acidity of the medium in which they have to operate. Most of the bacteria responsible for the decay of plant material are unable to flourish in acid conditions, even if the conditions are otherwise suitable. On the other hand, many of the fungi, including the wood-destroying fungi, are not so restricted, so that in acid soils micro-organic decomposition is mainly fungal.

These, then, are the physical and chemical conditions which allow decomposition to take place. Contrariwise, it follows that if these conditions do not obtain, decay will be prevented or at least slowed down, and this gives us a very useful guide as to the conditions which favour preservation. Time and again already we have had cause to refer to dryness and wetness as preservative factors; the dry tombs of Ancient Egypt on the one hand and the peat bogs of north-western Europe on the other. It is coincidental that we have here the two extremes of one factor – moisture – for the two conditions operate against the organisms of decay for quite different reasons. Extreme dryness operates simply through a shortage of that essential commodity – water. We meet this effect in our own lives, especially those of us who are householders. The best way to avoid dry rot is to keep the woodwork of a house well ventilated; the dry rot fungus is unable to attack the wood unless it is damp. The same is true of the wood-destroying beetles – comminuters *par excellence*. It appears that some of these animals (e.g. the death-watch beetle) feed not so much on the wood itself as on fungi which attack the wood, so that again, if timber is kept dry the fungus cannot thrive and the beetles are not interested.

Waterlogging, as in peat bogs, owes its preservative effect to the fact that in a waterlogged deposit air is excluded, so that the oxygen-rich atmosphere, essential for the well-being of animals and aerobic fungi and bacteria, is lacking. Under such conditions plant material may be preserved for thousands of years (though some biochemical changes may take place over long periods of time). In fact, the formation of peat itself is direct proof of such preservation. It should be realized, however, that this is only true if the waterlogging is permanent. If a bog dries out, perhaps seasonally, perhaps due to climatic change, then aerobic decomposition can take place, and once that has happened subsequent waterlogging, of course, cannot restore what has been destroyed, even though new peat growth may develop. So the history of the bog or swamp is important. This is more particularly true of neutral or alkaline peats (e.g. fen peats) than of acid peats (e.g. *Sphagnum* bogs), because a neutral or alkaline peat, once drained, is an extremely fertile material for biological growth; we have seen that bacterial growth, for instance, would be favoured by the low acidity. Acid peats, however, remain acid even after drainage, and this can exclude bacterial breakdown, though fungi may thrive.

It is rare for a major archaeological site to be preserved by water, but the tombs of Noin Ula in Russia are such a case.[123] They lie on the Selenga river which flows into Lake Baikal. After completion they filled up with water, which preserved such ephemeral materials as wood, woollen clothes and richly-worked tapestries, all in the most remarkable condition.

Similarly the archaeologist rarely meets a case where low temperature has been the main factor favouring preservation, but again Central Asia provided a good example. In the Altai Mountains the stone-topped tombs of the Pazyryk nomads became in effect ice houses through the development of ground ice under the mounds. The most perishable materials were preserved, including human bodies, their clothing, carpets, and many other objects. Even the colours remained in the designs of the carpets and wall draperies.[123]

The preservation of whole mammoths in the permanently frozen ground of Siberia provides direct information about the environment of these beasts, and indirectly this links up with the way of life of palaeolithic man. It is true that mammoths do not come in the category of plant remains and so are outside our subject, but the vegetation which they had been eating before death is also preserved in their stomachs and on their teeth and has given direct evidence of the plant environment in which they lived.[49]

So far we have considered only the normal environmental factors which affect preservation. There may, however, be special circumstances which can favour the preservation of organic remains in situations which otherwise would seem to contain no adverse factors for decay. A case of particular archaeological importance is the presence of injurious quantities of toxic metal components; copper is the most important example. It is particularly noticeable in some artefacts that where there have been copper or bronze fittings the organic material on which these occurred – perhaps wood or leather – was preserved in the immediate vicinity of the metal but had completely disappeared elsewhere (Biek, 1963). There seems no doubt that quite small concentrations of copper can prevent the activity of micro-organisms in conditions which are otherwise favourable to them. Here again there is a parallel with modern practice. Bordeaux mixture, which contains copper sulphate, is still widely used as a horticultural dressing against mildew and other fungal diseases. This explanation no doubt lies behind the fact that prehistoric copper mines, such as those of Austria,[127] have provided abundant remains of artefacts made of perishable materials – wood, leather, textiles – and so contributed greatly to our knowledge of everyday articles. In such circumstances the soil and deposits must be rich in toxic copper compounds. Salt mines, too, have proved rich sources of perishable goods, and here again micro-biological activity has been inhibited, this time by an exceptionally high salt content.

There are other situations, too, in which preservation is unexpectedly good even though the site is not waterlogged. For instance, remarkable preservation was found under Silbury Hill;[38] and pollen was recovered from garden soils buried beneath several metres of volcanic lapilli at Pompeii.[39] Perhaps such examples are to be explained in terms of anaerobic conditions developing beneath a massive overburden.

Another bacteriostatic effect which is becoming more widely recognized as of archaeological importance is that due to polyphenols. The most important of these may for our present purpose be grouped under the general heading of tannins. Occasionally it is found that organic materials such as leather placed in tree-trunk coffins – usually oak – are surprisingly well preserved; this appears to be due to the high content of tannins in oak wood, especially the heartwood. Recently a number of examples have come to light of the preservation of a variety of materials in waterlogged deposits which for one reason or another are rich in tannins. From one such deposit, at Vindolanda, the resting spores (endospores) of a bacterium *Thermoactinomyces* proved to be still viable, having apparently survived for 1,900 years.[142] Not only may perishable material such as wood and leather be preserved, but metal objects such as iron nails may be present in an almost uncorroded state. There is now a considerable amount of research going on into the behaviour of polyphenols by chemists, biologists and metallurgists. Some of the problems and questions of archaeological relevance are valuably discussed in *Archaeology and the Microscope* by Biek (1963). Polyphenols may be a contributory cause of the excellent preservative properties of peat bogs, which are usually attributed to the physical exclusion of oxygen. On the other hand, raw humus is a purely organic material which is well-drained and Iversen[83] has recorded one such deposit, at Draved, in Denmark, which spans a period of over three millennia. This is exceptional because raw humus is easily consumed by fire; apart from forest fires it was also cut and taken away for fuel, so that it seldom got the chance of persisting. The plant litters which form this particular type of humus are characteristically rich in polyphenols.

Physical impressions of plant material can be a most specific form of vegetation record, even though the actual material has itself disappeared. Cereal grain impressions in pottery have enabled Helbaek[68] to build up in remarkable detail a knowledge of crops and weeds in prehistoric times (see Chapter 10). Impressions are sometimes preserved on other materials too. For instance, I have seen perfectly recognizable impressions of bracken fronds on corroded bronze,[150] and impressions of wood grain have been found on leather objects. Plasterwork is also a useful source of plant casts, especially where it has incorporated grass or straw as a strengthener. But the most perfect casts I have seen have not been in an artificial material but in natural tufa. This is a calcareous deposit formed at springs of lime-rich water; where it drips or runs over leaves and stems these become completely encrusted. Eventually the plant parts die and decay, leaving impressions of exquisite detail. Where such deposits can be referred to a past hydrological state, such as the tufas in Sahara oases which indicate pluvial times, they may be of considerable if indirect importance to archaeology.

Coprolites, or fossilized faeces, are another source of ancient plant remains. They are usually preserved under arid conditions. Coprolites attributable to the extinct giant sloth have been studied in North America for both pollen and macroscopic plant remains,[108] and desiccated human coprolites have yielded valuable information on prehistoric diets.[22]

Microscopic coprolites, the faecal pellets of small soil arthropods, may persist for a long time. It has been shown, for instance, that such pellets in Dutch heath soils were produced by animals that lived there when the land was covered with oak forest.[92]

Much of our knowledge about early plants is due to the fact that very frequently plant remains became changed from their natural chemical state to elemental carbon; that is, they were carbonized. Elemental carbon is practically indestructible chemically (except by burning), and as it offers no source of sustenance to micro-organisms, it remains unchanged indefinitely. Frequently the original plant structure is preserved in great detail, as in charcoal, and identification of the original wood can be made from it (see Chapter 8). The same applies to other plant parts such as leaves or seeds, and this has contributed a great deal to our knowledge of the botanical side of early agriculture. The carbonization of grain has already been mentioned.

On this subject something must be said about the process of carbonization, by which I mean conversion to elemental carbon. We all recognize a large fragment of charcoal when we see it and accept the fact that this was transformed into the state in which we find it by incomplete combustion in a fire. This is a process we can see and carry out today. Yet one frequently finds people who believe that some carbonized plant material (grain is usually in mind) has got into that state by a slow process of ageing. Helbaek has refuted this idea very forcibly on a number of occasions (e.g. [68]), and there can be no doubt that he is right. As we have seen in this chapter dead plant material is immediately subject to the attack of many organisms which ultimately bring about complete decay. If this were not the case the earth would be littered with carbonized remains of earlier vegetation. In some of the special circumstances we have been discussing plant remains may be converted to a dark, perhaps hard condition (e.g. bog oak), but they have not become elemental carbon, and the process has no relevance to the carbonization of grain. Helbaek refers to the widely held idea of 'spontaneous combustion' by which is meant what I have called a slow process of ageing. True spontaneous combustion, of course, can occur, as when a rick of green hay ferments internally to such an extent that it builds up a high enough temperature to cause it to ignite. Indeed it has been suggested that it was through such combustion in his pile of bedding, perhaps grass or bracken, that man first discovered fire – a stimulating thought. But the point which must be emphasized here is that the result was a fire, and this may have produced some carbonized plant remains.

Well and badly grown oaks.

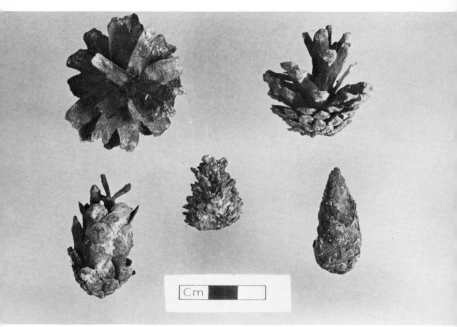

Pine cones from waterlogged deposit. Thatcham.

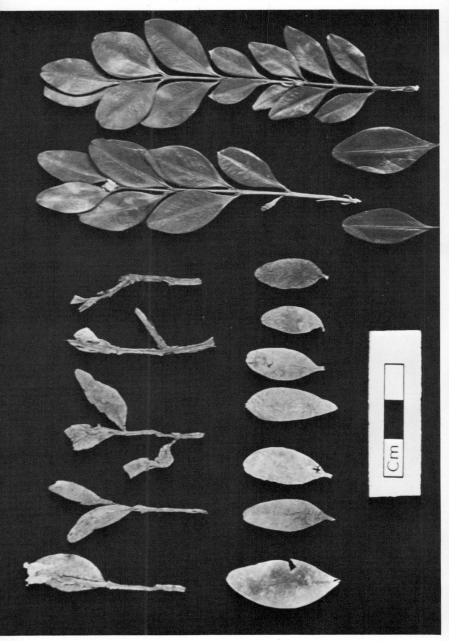

Box. Winterton.

Seeds. Beckford.

Seeds. Silbury.

Seeds. Cereals –
charred.

Moss.

1cm

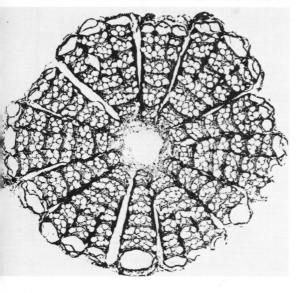

Transverse section of charcoal of Traveller's Joy. (*Clematis*)

ree rings.

a

b

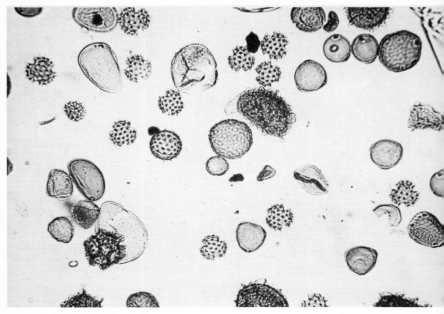

Modern pollen and spores.

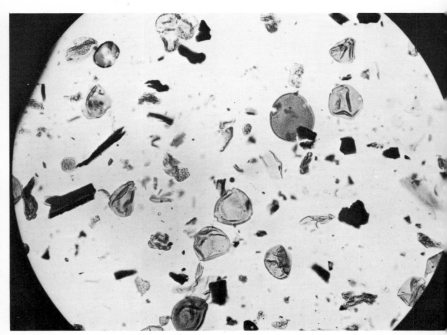

Old pollen and spores.

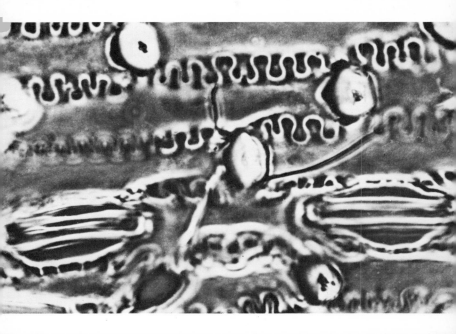

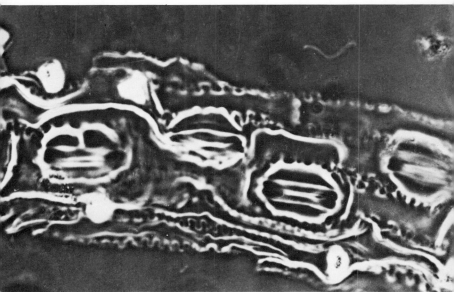

Silica skeletons.

Leaf impressions.

In nature, fire is essential for the conversion of plant material into elemental carbon.

Lest it still be felt that some site conditions, for instance under a protecting earthwork, may be different from those of the normal land surface, let us take a brief look at some of the early results from the two experimental earthworks built in southern England. These earthworks consisted of a bank about 7 m wide, 2 m high and 30 m long, together with a ditch from which the material was obtained. The object of the experiments was twofold: firstly to see how the bank and ditch weather over the next century or so, and secondly to see what happens to materials of archaeological significance buried in the bank and under the turf core. These materials included linen, cotton and wool cloth, billets of wood (oak and hazel) both charred on the surface and uncharred, bone, fresh and calcined, *Lycopodium* spores, and various inorganic objects such as pottery and flints. The original plan was to cut a section of the bank at 2, 4, 8, 16, 32, 64 and 128 years after construction and to recover the objects and materials buried. The first earthwork was built on chalk in 1960,[87] and the bank was sectioned in 1962, 1964 and 1976.[88] Even after two years considerable deterioration had taken place in the textiles, and in fact one piece of cotton could not be found. After four years, further deterioration could be traced. The wood, too, was showing measurable loss of weight due to attack by fungi, which could be seen penetrating the charred and uncharred billets alike; as far as the evidence goes so far, the surface charring does nothing to preserve the wood beneath. The distribution of the *Lycopodium* spores (chosen as being very resistant to decay) showed that they had moved both upward and downward, apparently through the agency of earthworms. Indeed, earthworms were found to be working right in the core of the bank, and moles had penetrated to the core to feed on them. In other words, even in the centre of this substantial bank there was no restriction on normal aerobic biological processes.

The second earthwork was constructed on heathland, on an acid infertile soil, deliberately chosen to contrast with the one on chalk. This was built in 1963, and in view of the loss of one of the cotton samples even in two years on the chalk, it was decided to make a section at one year in this case, even though it is to be expected that this would be a much less active soil biologically. This bank was therefore sectioned in 1964 and 1965 and again in 1968 and 1972. The cotton was not recovered in 1964 – it had already gone. Earthworms were not present in this acid medium, but vigorous faunal activity was again found, right in the centre of the

97

bank, this time in the shape of beetle larvae actively feeding on the organic material. It looks as though some reappraisal may be necessary of our concept of the poor biological activity under conditions of high acidity. This was particularly shown by the unexpectedly advanced state of decay shown by the wood billets buried beneath the turf stack in the core of the bank. In 1965 these samples were only recoverable with difficulty and in 1972 some could not be recovered. By contrast the decay of wood in the sandy make-up of the bank was much less advanced. Another feature introduced into this earthwork was the placing of copper discs on top of samples of textiles. Results already suggest some preservative influence of the copper (see p. 94 above).

From what has been said in this chapter it must be clear that although the agents of decay are so very widespread, there is a variety of conditions, applying to widely different climatic circumstances, in which plant remains can be preserved for the illumination of the archaeologist and his botanical colleague. We assume too readily that plant remains are not preserved. More often they are not expected, not looked for and therefore not found. Particularly must archaeologists outside the temperate zone re-assess the potentialities of their sites. The work on the origins of maize in Meso-America[106] shows what can be achieved by a full investigation, one not restricted by traditional blinkers. How much attention has been paid in the Old World to the botany of mud-brick? Adobe in the New World has been shown to contain plant remains, and pollen has now been found in countable quantities in mud-brick from Çatal Hüyük. Interpretation of the evidence may be difficult, but at least let us have the evidence. In succeeding chapters applications of the special aspects may suggest that we have been too defeatist and unimaginative in our approach to archaeological botany.

Nevertheless, archaeology has contributed a great deal to our knowledge of vegetation history. In his *History of the British Flora* Godwin (1975) itemizes the records for all species on which we have information, and in many cases the data come from archaeological sites. These finds are mainly of charcoal and carbonized fruits, but the enormous impact of pollen analysis and peat research, which rarely touches archaeology directly, has perhaps tended to overshadow the contribution of archaeology. Even so, an increased awareness of what botanical material sites may hold could lead to a marked increase in the contribution of archaeology to our knowledge of plant history. This would have fundamental scientific value in addition to its direct application to the sites themselves.

8

Wood

In this chapter wood is interpreted in the strictly botanical sense, the xylem of the secondarily thickened plant. Other tissues which also form part of the woody stem, such as bast or bark, will be dealt with in Chapter 10. A useful work of reference on this subject is Jane's *Structure of Wood* (1970).

The xylem or wood of a typical tree is produced by a single layer of actively growing (or meristematic) cells which completely encircles the stem (Fig. 3). These cells, called the cambium, divide parallel to the circumference, laying down juvenile wood cells on the inner side of this meristematic sheath. As these grow and differentiate the diameter of the trunk is increased, necessitating a certain amount of division of the cambium cells by radial cross-walls in order to keep pace with the expanding circumference. The wood serves two main functions and a number of minor ones, and its structure is closely related to these functions. The two main functions are mechanical support and conduction of water with its dissolved salts. For the first of these, the cellulose walls of the cells are reinforced with lignin. Once the cell has reached its full size a complete deposit of lignin is laid down over the whole wall, the cell dying in the process. These cells, wood fibres, may be greatly elongated; in fact they may force their way between their neighbours by a process called sliding growth. The conducting tissues also tend to have an elongated form, as one might expect. Long cells similar to fibres, but connecting with each other through pits in their side and end walls, are called tracheids. In softwoods, that is, the woods of coniferous trees, tracheids form the sole means of water movement up the tree. In hardwoods, however, there are vessels, larger in diameter than tracheids or fibres – sometimes large enough to be seen with the naked eye in a cross-section – and these consist of long chains of cells from which the end walls have disappeared, leaving an unobstructed tube. In some species end walls do persist, but these are perforated by holes or slots – multiple perforation plates – quite distinct in appearance from the smaller pits between tracheids. These multiple perforation plates, as we shall see, may leave recognizable traces in some deposits.

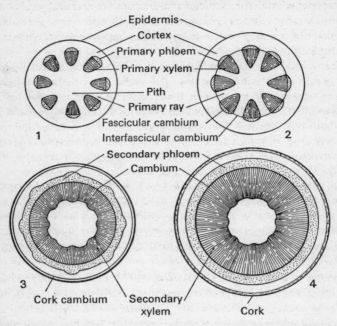

3. The development of the cylinder of wood as a twig ages (diagrammatic).
By permission of the Edinburgh University Press, from Alan Brook's *The Living Plant*

All the wood tissues so far described are dead. But the outer zone of the wood cylinder, the sapwood, is not a totally dead tissue through which water moves by purely physical forces. Truth to tell, in this age of sophisticated science, we still do not know how water does reach the top of a tree, but life processes are certainly involved. Living cells with undifferentiated walls, called parenchyma, are present throughout the sapwood. Sometimes they are scattered or diffuse, sometimes aggregated into clusters or bands, or grouped around the vessels. In fact the arrangement of these cells is of importance in the identification of different species from the wood. One of their functions may be to store starch for the next season's growth; the trunk of a tree is its principal storage organ. In the heartwood these cells are dead, but one of their last functions is probably the deposition of waste products. The heartwood is often distinct in colour from the sapwood, due to the polyphenols (tannins) and other substances consigned to this, the tree's dustbin. We have already seen that oak heartwood, for example, is a rich source of tannins, and another practical result is that the heartwood is relatively resistant to decay, though even it is unable to withstand the attack of certain fungi such as butt-rots which convert the tree trunk into a hollow cylinder.

When a twig first starts to lay down the ring of wood it usually has a pith – a soft-celled living tissue (Fig. 3). Contact between this living tissue and the tissues on the outside of the cylinder of wood is maintained by radial strips of cells called medullary rays. As the twig enlarges the pith dies, but radial lifelines through the wood are still necessary, and many new rays arise as the diameter increases. These rays consist mainly of parenchymatous cells, but some may also have tracheids in them, pointing to a function of radial transport through the wood. The living ray cells, like the wood parenchyma, may also store starch. Rays vary a great deal in size, shape and detailed structure; they may sometimes be aggregated into giant rays as in oak or hazel. The structure of rays is of prime diagnostic importance in identification, often necessitating microscopic examination in transverse (TS), tangential longitudinal (TLS) and radial longitudinal sections (RLS).

These are the essential features of wood. There may be other characteristics in some timbers. For instance, resin canals are present in many (not all) conifers, running radially along the rays as well as vertically through the wood. Latex vessels and oil ducts are likewise characteristic of some woods, and one could enlarge on many special arrangements and adaptations. A feature which is occasionally of archaeological importance is the structure of the wood of climbers. A regular cylinder of wood clearly would not have the flexibility required by climbers – a flexibility which makes them particularly useful to man. It is achieved by the wood being laid down in large strands separated by soft tissues.

Those beginning a study of wood structure with a view to the identification of wood frequently find that the unknown samples fail to match up closely with the named samples. An unknown specimen may be keyed out with little difficulty, but when compared with reference material it looks so different that one doubts one's diagnosis. This may be partly due to the inevitable variability in wood. This variability does not involve the basic structure of the wood, but rather the manifestation of that structure. If a tree is growing fast, the cells will be numerous and relatively thin-walled;

if slow, fewer and thick-walled. This produces the growth rings so familiar in cut timber; in tropical trees whose growth is continuous throughout the year there are no growth rings. But apart from this, different specimens of the same species may be growing under very different ecological conditions, so that one is putting on wood at a great rate and another hardly at all. Inevitably the microscopic appearance of the wood will differ markedly, though the structural units will remain basically the same. Even in the same tree we can expect differences. The wood of a twig may look superficially very different from a piece of the trunkwood of the same tree. As reference collections are nearly always of timber, twig identification can be particularly difficult – and archaeological samples of charcoal are much more frequently of twig than of timber.

One aspect of variation which has received too little attention is the difference between root and stem wood; I believe this accounts for many difficulties in identifying archaeological samples, particularly of charcoal. In describing the structure of wood it was shown how the structure related to function, and in certain respects the function of the root is different from that of the stem. The root has not got to stand the enormous compression which is imposed on the trunk of a tall tree; rather it has to withstand tension, like an anchor line. Roots are therefore not only less massive than stems and branches, but their fibre cells are often larger and less heavily thickened. Growth rings also may be absent or irregular, rays less conspicuous, and the vessel pattern different from the stem. This was brought home to me forcibly when examining a section of oak root; the large vessels which impart the characteristic appearance to oak wood were totally lacking. Differences are not usually as gross as this, but clearly confusion is sometimes possible.

Foresters and timber users are familiar with the fact that even in the aerial portions of the tree the forces acting on the tree will vary. A leaning tree will be sustaining compression of the trunk on one side and tension on the other, so that when it is sawn longitudinally serious warping may occur as the forces are released. In branches this double force pattern is inevitable. The tree reacts to such situations by adding extra wood where necessary, and in this connection it is interesting to note the difference in behaviour of conifers and hardwoods. If a section is cut of a horizontal branch it will be seen that in each case the ring pattern is eccentric; but in the conifer the extra wood will have been laid down beneath the original centre, and in the hardwood above it. This is due to the fact that the wood of hardwoods is strong in compression but weak in tension, whilst in conifers the reverse is true. We have already seen that the compression wood of pine branches was selected in prehistoric times for making skis.

It is not the intention here to provide keys for the identification of wood. There are excellent books and card keys available for this purpose (*Forest Products Research Bulletins* Nos 22, 25, 26) and as will be apparent by now, the job is not one for the inexperienced. Regrettably archaeological literature is rich in incorrect identifications already, showing that even botanists are liable to err unless they have made a special study of wood structure. Identification is ideally made on the microscope, on TS, RLS and TLS sections as already described. For the separation of some woods high power magnification is essential, as with some of the conifers; here the detailed structure and arrangement of pits between the cells are of diagnostic importance. In other cases the important features are of a coarser dimension and can be distinguished with a ×10 hand lens (Fig. 4). Punched card keys have been prepared for both microscope and lens identification of the important commercial timbers of the world. However, for our purpose the scope of such keys is not always wide enough. Our specimen of charcoal may derive from a shrub which does not form timber at all, let alone commercial timber. Here we have to depend on our own reference material.

The distribution of the vessels is perhaps the most characteristic feature of a wood specimen seen in transverse section – that is, assuming that it has vessels;[2] if not, then it is coniferous (Fig. 4c). The vessels may be arranged in rings, when the pattern is known as ring-porous (Fig. 4a), or they may be more evenly scattered through the wood, that is, diffuse porous (Fig. 4b). Sometimes they have more than one pattern. In oak, for example, very large vessels are arranged in a ring-porous pattern, but smaller ones occur in long radial groups or flares; in elm the larger vessels are similarly arranged, but smaller ones are grouped in tangential bands. In the diffuse-porous woods there are many patterns ranging from long radial strings of vessels (e.g. hazel) to completely solitary ones.

The next most obvious feature is the ray pattern. Are the rays wide or narrow (or both)? And how deep? Are the cells all the same (homogeneous) or are the outer cells different in shape (heterogeneous)? – a microscopic feature this. Then we want to know how the parenchyma is distributed – this was discussed earlier; and the pattern of pits on the vessel walls may be important – another feature needing the microscope. And so on.

There does not seem to be much the archaeologist can do about all this – it is a job for the expert. But sometimes there is. It should be possible for anyone to recognize the main features of oak – the large pores (vessels) in a ring, the flares of smaller vessels and the occasional huge multiseriate ray. These are quite diagnostic. If the archaeologist in Britain, for instance, could recognize oak when he saw it, he could greatly reduce the amount of material needing to be submitted to the botanist. Many collections of charcoal have I ploughed through, to report at the end – all oak. It is the

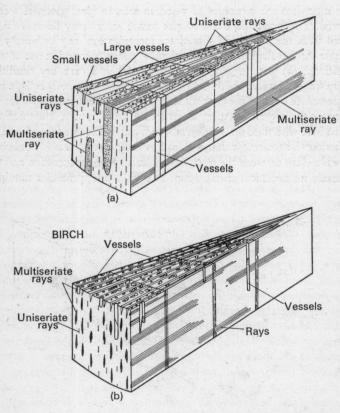

4. The structure of three different types of wood as seen in

commonest species found in British charcoal, and one of the least informative ecologically or chronologically. Moreover, if the archaeologist could recognize oak, he would not have to wait endlessly for the specialist's report. I would not extend this advice to cover any other species, even those relatively easy to identify. There is none as straightforward as oak, and other species may be of such ecological importance that there must be no doubt of the identification. Moreover, all three characters mentioned above must be present in the same specimen; if the aggregate rays are missing, for example, the specimen *may* be sweet chestnut (*Castanea*). In all cases of doubt, and in all cases of diffuse-porous wood, the material should be submitted to an expert.

So much for the structure of wood as seen in ideal material – fresh material. The wood the archaeologist comes across may be very far removed from this ideal, and sometimes identification may be simply impossible. Archaeological wood specimens are usually found in one of three conditions: (*a*) waterlogged; (*b*) charcoal; (*c*) in a very dry condition. Rarely traces of wood are found in freely-drained but moist soils, e.g. in postholes. As each of these conditions poses different problems for the excavator and for the botanist, let us look at each in turn. I am not concerned here with the conservation of wooden artefacts but merely with the extraction and treatment that will lead to their identification. Sometimes there is a clash between the treatment necessary for conservation and that necessary for botanical examination; in such a case, priorities should be

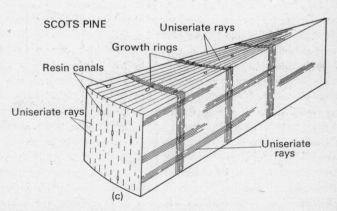

transverse, radial longitudinal and tangential longitudinal sections.

resolved beforehand. More often, however, the clash comes in a different way. The artefact has been 'conserved' and then the question arises as to what wood it is made of. It is sent to the botanist with strict instructions that it must not be damaged in any way. We have seen the sort of criteria on which identification depends; it will be apparent that the botanist has only one option in these circumstances – to send the object back.

This sort of problem arises most frequently in category (a), waterlogged wood, which is especially difficult for the conservationist because such wood, if it is allowed to dry out, may become so distorted that the artefact is scarcely worth preserving. If decomposition is too far gone, the object may have lost all internal cohesion, calling for very special conservation treatment. The botanist, too, is interested in preserving the object as far as possible in its original shape, but he does not want the fine structure to be clogged up with intractable preservatives which will prevent identification. Almost invariably waterlogged wood must be sectioned for identification; the saturated material is too spongy to allow a surface to be prepared for lens examination, and if it is allowed to dry it shrinks so much that the diagnostic features cannot be seen. When fresh wood is sectioned on a microtome it is usually rigid enough to stand up to the knife and so allow a thin section to be cut. Ancient waterlogged wood will seldom permit this, so it has to be embedded to give it rigidity. As it cannot be dried out those standard botanical embedding agents which are non-aqueous (e.g. paraffin wax) cannot be used. There are, however, aqueous waxes (e.g. Carbowax) which serve very well. The embedding is a slow tedious business, best carried out in the laboratory, so the archaeologist's task is to get the wood to the laboratory still in a waterlogged state. With polythene bags and containers as standard equipment this offers no problem. Once the wood is embedded in wax of the right consistency – a range of grades is available in these waxes – it can be sectioned in the normal manner. Very often the wood is strongly permeated with a brown organic deposit, but this may be removed by passing the sections through hypochlorite before mounting. If the wood is badly deteriorated the middle lamella, that is the unlignified common wall between cells, may have broken down so that the cells lose their cohesion. In these circumstances a microscope section may be virtually impossible to obtain. The excavator must be understanding if he sends a botanist what looks like a perfectly good, if rather wet, piece of wood and is told that identification is impossible. His frustration will be matched by that of the botanist who has spent days or weeks carefully embedding this wretched material.

Charcoal is found in archaeological sites of all ages and areas. It, too, has its own special problems to offer; in fact some wood anatomists will not touch it. It cannot be sectioned by normal means; all the cell walls have been converted to carbon, whether they were originally lignified or not, and it is always shrunken and often badly distorted. Yet most people seeing a piece of charcoal under the microscope for the first time are struck with wonder that the cell structure is preserved in such beautiful detail considering what it has been through. It is indeed remarkable, and one's amazement increases when, under the high power microscope, it is possible to see cell thickenings and pits in all their intricate detail. The problem is to be able to see these details in a material that has become black and opaque through carbonization. Incident light has to be used instead of transmitted light as in the case of wood sections. Normally a fresh fractured surface is examined at a magnification of ×10 to ×20; in favourable material magnifications as high as ×100 are sometimes possible.[100] Recently an improvement on the technique has allowed the examination of transverse or longitudinal surfaces at magnifications as high as ×400. By grinding the faces on emery paper and cleaning them with a blast of compressed air, a level clear surface is obtained which can easily be traversed on the mechanical stage of the microscope. (See page 5 of illustrated section.)

Material which easily crumbles presents problems. One means of dealing with it is to embed it in resin and then grind it to a thin section as though it were a rock or pottery sample. With practice sections can be made thin enough to see much of the essential detail, but the method is laborious and not easily applied to longitudinal sections. It has also proved possible to recognize microscopical detail in pulverized charcoal, and Paulssen (1964) has developed a method based on the pattern of pits which, within certain limits, enables identification of certain types of wood to be made.

Charcoal can vary a great deal in the condition in which it comes out of the site. Sometimes it is extremely friable, sometimes quite sound, depending, presumably, on how complete the process of carbonization was. It may be completely impregnated with lime or other deposits and sometimes it is tied together with living roots not only surrounding it but actually penetrating the vessels. Occasionally one comes across charcoal which appears at first sight to have an irregular pattern of large vessels, but these turn out to be an infestation of some wood-boring insect. In fact, I once split open a piece of charcoal and found a neolithic woodworm in it.

Excavators are often in some doubt as to whether charcoal is worth submitting for identification, perhaps because the fragments are too small. May I be allowed to offer a few suggestions from the botanist's point of view? First of all, do not select the specimens to be sent; if there is charcoal there, and its identity is of potential interest, send the whole lot. By selecting the bigger pieces a subjective element is being introduced, for the bigger pieces may be of one species and the smaller ones something quite different which happens to fragment more easily. There is no hard-and-fast rule as to minimum size – so much depends on the species involved and the features which a small piece happens to show. Sometimes a fragment less than 5 mm diameter can be identified with as much certainty as a piece 2 or 3 cms across; other times such a small piece is quite useless. Frequently in an excavation a large piece of charcoal is found, but it breaks up on extraction. Please do not throw this into the bag with all the other specimens, but pack it separately and label it as comprising one specimen. In this way the botanist only needs to make one identification instead of one on each fragment, which could run into a dozen or more. Charcoal specimens should be packed carefully in wadding or tissue so that they do not rattle about in transit. The practice of packing it in sand or soil is on the whole not successful. Sand tends to pack down with shaking, thus allowing movement, so that the recipient opens packets containing charcoal which has been pulverized by the loose sand. Finally, it is not worth trying to separate charcoal from mineral matter by flotation. It can work if the charcoal is in good condition, but if not the pieces fall apart. I once received for identification a bag full of what appeared to be wet soot.

It is not unusual in identifying charcoal to come across various extraneous materials. There may be other plant remains such as fruits, seeds, bark and so on, dealt with in Chapter 10. Fragments of carbonized wood pitch or perhaps resin, can look very like charcoal until they are examined under the microscope. Other alien substances include coal, bone and, perhaps the most frequent, small fragments of pottery.

Wood that has not been carbonized, but has been preserved in a dry environment can often be identified by using the normal botanical techniques, either for low or high magnification. It is to be expected that the wood will have shrunk considerably as it dried, and this can result in its becoming so hard that it is difficult to section on a microtome. Again the technique of grinding a thin section – in this case without embedding – can sometimes be used. In other circumstances the wood may have become so denatured that it is liable to powder, in which case embedding is essential, but once more it should be stressed that any technique carried out in the field should not preclude later botanical investigation.

From time to time remains of uncarbonized wood are found in earthworks and soils in freely-drained but damp conditions. Decomposition is always advanced, usually the evidence of timber being no more than a stain in the soil. Where actual wood remains are found (as they were at Woodhenge) it is a matter of luck whether identification will be possible. Fungal decay causes disorganization of the tissues by attacking the middle lamella, as we have already seen, so obliterating diagnostic features. Nevertheless, traces may be left which can be significant. For instance, multiple perforation plates (see p. 100) may be recognizable under the microscope, pointing to a certain group of species and definitely excluding others; in conifers, the type of pitting may similarly restrict the field of choice. In soil preparations for pollen analysis I have come across what appear to be casts of perforation plates. So far I have been unable to find out how they are formed, but again they may be of diagnostic interest, especially where found with pollen. It has also been shown that these plates, as well as fibres and tracheids, may contain sufficient silica that they remain recognizable even after the wood has been ashed.[24] This opens an interesting line of archaeological research with the microscope.

It was mentioned in the last chapter that impressions of wood can be found, for instance in plaster. Unfortunately the longitudinal cast of a piece of wood has no real diagnostic value. One often gets the impression that the species was, say, oak, but it is very unlikely that firm proof could be obtained unless actual fragments of the wood are also preserved. A rather special case of this is found in situations where there is a high lime content, resulting in the encasement of the wood in lime; in the course of time the lime can completely replace the wood, which decays away. One is left then with a piece of porous lime which looks exactly like wood to the naked eye, but shows none of the necessary detail under the lens or microscope. However, it has proved possible in such cases to dissolve the lime away with acid and recover enough microscopical material to prove the presence of wood and even, in fortunate circumstances, to identify the species concerned. Sometimes wood buried in a calcareous matrix can become petrified. In one such case only the outer layer of a beam retained the appearance of wood, but in thin section it was found that though the organic material had rotted away, the actual cell pattern was perpetuated in calcium carbonate, so permitting identification. Recently it has been shown that the microscopic detail of wood elements may be preserved as casts in iron corrosion deposits.[94]

In the first part of this book it has been shown how innumerable were the uses of wood to prehistoric man, so it is only to be expected that the remains of wood found in archaeological sites must reflect those uses to a large extent. Yet the choice of species used was not always predetermined by the use to which the wood was to be put. Sometimes any wood would do; this could apply, for instance, to a fire. Consequently the species used might reflect the availability of those species in the surrounding neighbourhood. It is difficult to know when this argument is justified and when it is not; it may be necessary to seek corroborative evidence, for example from pollen analysis. Nevertheless, wood remains constitute a potential source of environmental information which should be thoroughly tested and explored. Deductions from the wood specimens themselves seem to be more promising at first sight than they really are. It has been suggested that the closeness of the rings in a piece of charcoal gives us information about the rate of growth and that this could have ecological implications. But unless we are dealing with a tree-stump *in situ* we cannot relate the specimen to its site. In any landscape there are good sites and bad, well-grown trees and poor, and even in the same tree widely spaced rings and narrow – as on the topside and underside of the same branch. There are too many ifs and buts to make this approach generally useful. Even experts may take totally different views of the same material. This happened with the charcoal from Maiden Castle. Some experts said that because the charcoal fragments were all of small dimension it could be concluded that only small-sized trees and shrubs grew on the chalk in the Iron Age.[136] Others argued that in making a fire and stoking it the larger stems and branches were fed into the fire butt first, the large-diameter wood being consumed and only small-sized branches and twigs remaining to form charcoal at the edge of the fire.[58] The only safe conclusion is that these charcoals tell us nothing about the size of the trees and shrubs on the chalk hills – if indeed there were any.

It is for reasons such as this that specialist reports on archaeological wood specimens are seldom more than lists of names. If, however, the excavator has some reason, other than the accumulation of facts, for submitting wood specimens for analysis, it would make the analysis so much more pointed if the botanist could be told of it. This plea has already been made by Miss Western[174] and I should like to add my support. I am sure this would lead to more interesting specialist reports and more integration with the excavation report.

It is not proposed here to discuss wood, charcoal, or any other plant remains as material for radiocarbon dating, though brief reference will be made to the subject in Chapter 13. In the archaeologist's own interests, however, he should always inform the wood specialist that the material is eventually going to be needed for dating. By doing so he is protecting his material against the (remote) chance of contamination or loss. Nobody handling the material should be left in the dark.

9

Pollen and spores

It may not be immediately obvious why such microscopic bodies as pollen and spores should warrant a chapter to themselves; but such is their contribution to our knowledge of past vegetation that they could be – and indeed have been – the subject of whole books. If one compares the very imperfect ideas which were held on the history of the British flora at the beginning of the century (that is, before pollen analysis was known) with what we know now, the difference is staggering. This revolutionary change is due to the surprising fact that of all the parts of the plant pollen grains are the most resistant to decomposition, in spite of the fact that they play a quite ephemeral role in the life of the plant.

The identification of pollen grains can rarely be absolutely specific, unlike that of seeds and fruits. Usually it is possible to ascribe a pollen grain to its family, quite often to a genus, but only exceptionally to species. Of course, where there is only one native species in a genus we may make a reasonably safe guess: an ivy pollen grain in British deposits is almost certainly *Hedera helix*; a holly grain, *Ilex aquifolium*. But errors could creep in, especially if there have been big climatic changes since the deposit under investigation was laid down. Identification of pollen grains is possible because of the enormous range in size and structure which pollen can exhibit. (See page 6 of illustrated Section.) Again, this seems totally unrelated to function; a bast fibre cell of nettle only differs from one of lime in size, but their pollen grains are totally different; a wood tracheid of larch is almost identical with one from spruce, but their pollen grains are quite dissimilar.

By its very nature pollen is more widespread than any other part of the plant; indeed it can be both an advantage and a disadvantage that it can be found far from the plant which produced it; an advantage because pollen can be carried to places where it can be preserved, such as peat bogs, without which our knowledge of the past would be so much poorer. At the same time it is difficult to tell exactly where the pollen has come from, and this constitutes a real drawback to ecological interpretation. Because pollen analysis first started and has largely developed in peaty materials and other waterlogged deposits, it is commonly believed that it can be found only under these conditions. As a result archaeology has undoubtedly suffered, because few people have looked for pollen in other contexts. Consider the release and dispersal of pollen. The great bulk of species are either wind-pollinated (anemophilous) or insect-pollinated (entomophilous); a few are water-pollinated, and some are even pollinated by birds or, like the *Aspidistra* – its flowers arise at soil level – by snails and slugs. Wind-pollination is clearly rather a chancy business, and nature overcomes this by producing a great amount of pollen; anemophilous plants therefore tend to be over-represented in pollen analyses. Entomophily is a much more controlled process, and usually the pollen production of species pollinated in this way is low and dispersal is related to the flight range of the insects rather than to the wider movements of air. There are some species which seem to form a half-way stage between anemophily and entomophily – plants whose flowers are adapted to attract insects, but also seem to contribute to the air-borne pollen. Heather (*Calluna*) is an outstanding example, but this also seems to be true of lime (*Tilia*) and probably some members of the Compositae.

During the flowering season the air is laden to a greater or lesser degree with pollen; the amount depends, as sufferers from hay fever will know, on whether the air is dry or humid. Most of this pollen settles out again within a few hundred yards from its source, but some remains in suspension and may be carried long distances before it settles. It is commonly assumed that the direction of furthest dispersal will be in the direction of the prevailing wind during the flowering season, and up to a point evidence confirms this. But it has also been shown that freak effects due to the movements of air masses by convection are not unusual, particularly along the shores of large sheets of water, and that surprising concentrations of pollen can occur as a result. Although pollen analysis has been so widely used in the past thirty or forty years, it is only recently that comprehensive investigations have been made to evaluate the influence of atmospheric factors on pollen deposition. Some information has been obtained by foresters and hay-fever specialists, but seldom by pollen analysts themselves. Nevertheless, the far-reaching consistency of results suggests that the influence of atmosphere variation was not sufficient to produce more than a minor variation in the pollen rain. Special cases may arise, as for instance when tree pollen coming from a long distance is falling on ground itself covered by forest; then the quantity of transported pollen is insignificant in comparison with that being shed by the vegetation on the site.

Whatever its source, pollen showers down upon every exposed surface within reach: fields, woods, roads, rooftops, lakes and the sea, and even on the ice of glaciers and ice-sheets. But only a limited number of such collecting areas are of any value for pollen analysis. For pollen analysis to be possible, whether it is meaningful or not, the pollen has to be preserved; or rather, the destruction of pollen has to be slowed down or stopped. Although pollen is destroyed with more difficulty than other plant parts, it is not, of course, immune to decay and under certain conditions can decay very rapidly. The living contents of the grains are usually quickly destroyed, before any visible change takes place in the wall of the pollen grain. Even animals such as bees, which feed on pollen, only digest the cell contents; the walls are excreted apparently unchanged. Earthworms may ingest pollen as they feed in the soil, but it emerges unchanged in the cast. However, pollen walls can be attacked by aerobic bacteria and destroyed without difficulty, so preservation is most complete where conditions are the least favourable for aerobic bacteria. We have already met some of these when discussing the preservation of other plant remains. Any waterlogged deposit prevents aerobic bacterial action because the supply of oxygen is inadequate. Peats and lake muds are therefore very favourable to pollen preservation as long as they remain waterlogged. Bacteria need an adequate supply of moisture in order to live actively and where this is lacking they are unable to bring about decomposition. This is why pollen can be found in arid soils and in recent years pollen analysis of semi-deserts has yielded astonishing results.[107] Bacterial activity is also suspended under cold conditions and consequently pollen may be recovered from arctic or alpine soils and deposits; pollen analyses have even been carried out on the ice layers of glaciers. All these conditions – wetness, dryness and cold – are also somewhat inhibiting to human life too, so the relevance of such sites to archaeology is limited. There is one other factor, however, which can militate strongly against bacterial activity even at optimum conditions of aeration, temperature and moisture: this is acidity. Most aerobic bacteria are unable to function if the environment is – or becomes – too acid. Consequently it has been possible to extend pollen analysis to many archaeological sites on acid soils (Dimbleby, 1962), which are common in north-temperate regions, and there is some indication that even in the tropics pollen may be found if conditions are acid enough.

On the debit side this leaves us with the fertile soils where drainage is good and acidity is low – soils which today are the mainstay of agriculture and often were so even in prehistoric times. In particular it rules out the chalk, which is of such prehistoric importance, though occasionally useful pollen data have been obtained from chalk sites.[41, 95] Pollen breakdown is so rapid in such soils that if any pollen is found, for instance in a buried soil, it is likely to be contemporary with the burial of that soil.

These then are the conditions under which pollen may be preserved; but even if it is found and can be extracted it does not necessarily follow that it can be made to tell a useful story. If pollen is laid down year by year in successive layers, without any movement from one to the other, then it is possible to trace the sequence of changes in pollen deposition over the ages (Faegri and Iversen, 1975). In particular, if these changes can be related to outside causes such as climate, which took place at known times, then the pollen sequence itself can be used as an indirect method of dating. This will be discussed more fully in Chapter 13. The conditions necessary for ideal stratification of pollen are only found in specialized situations, particularly under waterlogged conditions: peat bogs, in which the peat is progressively growing upwards, are the most frequently used, but muds accumulating at the bottom of lakes can also serve in this way. We have seen, however, that pollen can be preserved under many other conditions, and these may provide some degree of stratification – not as complete, perhaps, as in peat bogs or lake deposits – which enables broad changes to be recognized. This is possible, for instance, in certain soils, notably acid ones in which earthworms and other soil animals which mix the humus layers are absent.[35] These do not give absolute stratification, but in the course of time the oldest pollen finds its way to the lower part of the soil profile and above it progressively younger pollen is found until at the surface the pollen is mainly recent. We still do not understand the mechanism of this process, but this does not detract from its usefulness; nor does the fact that the results it gives are not as clear-cut as those from properly stratified deposits. In fact, these different media of preservation, by their inherent nature, give somewhat different results and are in a sense complementary to one another. A peat bog, for instance, receives its pollen from the landscape surrounding the bog, a landscape which may be a mosaic of vegetation types. The pollen sequence in a soil, however, is derived very largely from the vegetation growing on that soil; it will represent only one of the mosaic patches which contribute to the peat-bog pattern, so that in a varied landscape there will rarely be close similarity between contemporary pollen spectra from a peat bog and from an adjacent soil. This useful fact is overlooked by those pollen analysts who, distrustful of anything which is not absolutely stratified, will only accept evidence which comes from, or can be related to, peat or lake deposits.

This distinction has considerable importance to archaeology, because the conditions of ideal pollen preservation are rarely ideal for human settlement. It is true that time and again we have referred to artefacts preserved in peat bogs, but these are rarely associated with actual sites of settlement. There are very important exceptions: Star Carr,[27] and the Swiss pile-dwellings (Tschumi, 1949), for instance. In Denmark temporary sites – presumably summer camps, for the peat would be saturated in winter – have been fitted into the pollen sequence.[162] But in general men prefer to live on dry land, and any link between their environment, as reflected by pollen, and the peat bog must be indirect. Furthermore, as soon as man settles anywhere he inevitably modifies the vegetation around him. This fact in itself is of great ecological importance and from the nature of the changes we may be able to deduce what man was doing at the time. Pollen analysis of the site itself can give an answer for that site – an answer that may be correlatable with other site characters such as soil; a peat analysis cannot give such information for any specific site, but only for a 'region'.

Perhaps in north-western Europe we tend to take too parochial a view of pollen analysis. Even in Britain many archaeological sites – probably the majority – are far away from a peat bog or other suitable deposit for pollen analysis, and this is generally true when one considers archaeology over a much wider geographical range. The recent work of Martin and his colleagues in the south-western United States has shown that pollen analysis can be used with remarkable success under semi-arid conditions.[107] He has established pollen sequences through deep aggraded deposits resulting from erosion phases and his work has suggested that some of the commonly accepted ideas of the relationship between erosion and climate are erroneous. Pollen analysis is not a cut-and-dried procedure, only applicable under certain conditions. We have seen the wide range of conditions which permit pollen preservation, and we must use our ingenuity to make use of this fact. This is not to belittle the difficulties which can arise. The problem of contamination, for instance, is a very real one in imperfectly stratified deposits; it can even occur in more conventional circumstances. In particular, the chance of pollen of an earlier period becoming mixed with pollen of later origin is a danger for which we must be continually on the alert (Faegri and Iversen, 1975). The archaeologist is seldom in a position to recognize such a source of error, but he may be brought up against it if his pollen analyst refuses to give a report on a site which in all other aspects appears suitable.

Pollen analysis has been applied in so many ways to so many archaeological investigations that it is not possible here to do more than pick out a number of different settings and circumstances in which the method has been applied.

Mention has just been made of the situation in which cultural levels occur stratified in peat or lake sediments. In such a case the site can be approximately dated by pollen. However, pollen zones may be as much as 2,000 years in duration, though in a peat sequence the archaeological level may be located near the beginning or the end of the period and so narrowing the possible age range. This point should be remembered when dealing with isolated artefacts in a bog. It is possible to carry out a pollen analysis on them after removal (unless they have been too thoroughly cleaned), but a more precise result may be obtained if a series of samples above, at and below the object are taken for pollen analysis before it is removed from its peaty setting. Ideally this should be done by a specialist who can also make observations on the nature of the peat itself, but this may not always be possible. Whilst on the subject of individual artefacts rather than cultural levels stratified in peat or mud, it should be recognized that heavy objects, particularly of metal, are liable to have sunk through the peat before it had become consolidated. Their dating, therefore, may not be precise, but should be regarded as a *terminus post quem*. In the case of bog burials, in which the grave has been cut into the peat, the same applies though for a rather different reason.[139] In this case the upper edge of the grave may be marked in some way, perhaps by peat texture, which would enable a more precise date to be adduced.

In dealing with archaeological material in a stratified setting it has been traditional to think of pollen analysis primarily as a means of establishing date. Over the last two decades, however, the technique of radiocarbon dating has become established,[11] so that pollen analysis is no longer the chief means of dating; indeed, with facilities for radiocarbon dating so much more available – analysis can now be done commercially – this dating role of pollen analysis will play a progressively smaller part in archaeology, particularly if the present high cost of radiocarbon determinations can be brought within reach of unsubsidized excavators. But the information which pollen analysis gives about contemporary vegetation cannot be achieved by any other means. It has already been pointed out that bogs and lakes, collecting pollen as they do from an unspecified area, have their limitations in this respect. Nevertheless, a great deal can be learnt: the influence of the Swiss lake-dwellers on the surrounding forest was detectable in the pollen analyses;[160] the deforestation of the Breckland in East Anglia was demonstrated by the pollen sequences in Hockham Mere; [57] and more recently the impact of early agriculture, from the first temporary clearings to the later complete and permanent clearance, has been demonstrated by close-sampled analyses of peat bogs in widely different parts of Britain.[166] Although we may not be able to say exactly what was happening at any given place, we can say with precision just when the observed ecological phases existed. It was this sort of study, pioneered by Iversen over 30 years ago, which first gave us the term 'landnam', the phase of forest clearance for agriculture which is so characteristic of the spread of neolithic man.[81] The effect can be recognized and dated from pollen profiles even though no associated artefacts are found. So great is the 'landnam' effect in so many pollen profiles that it is extraordinary that it went unrecognized for so long. Perhaps pollen analysts had been more concerned with dating, which depends mainly upon the tree pollen, and had devoted relatively little attention to the pollen of grasses and herbs and the pioneer shrubs which colonized land cleared for agriculture. Now we are even beginning to recognize evidence of local and temporary clearings made by mesolithic man,[135, 145, 149] (see Chapter 11).

In north-western Europe there are many archaeological sites which are buried beneath peat today but which lie on the land surface beneath the peat. As they are not actually stratified in peat, they cannot be put into their appropriate period by pollen analysis of the peat itself. On the Pennine Hills mesolithic sites can be found immediately beneath the peat;[62] in Ireland it may be a Bronze Age or even neolithic site.[129] In each case the peat may have been formed during the last 2,000 years, so that the base of it gives us no clue as to the actual age of the sites beneath it, nor any indication of ecological conditions at the time of occupation by whatever culture had left its artefacts. There may have been a gap of 3,000 years, 300 years or 3 years between the occupation and the onset of peat formation; pollen analysis of the peat cannot tell us, though pollen analysis of the buried soil itself may give some indication. It has already been pointed out that a soil, if acid enough, may yield a pollen profile which gives a broad picture of changes in vegetation. Nevertheless there are drawbacks in this approach·

when it comes to filling gaps in the time scale. One is that erosion of the upper layers of the soil may have taken place, so obliterating part of the record; this will depend partly upon the topography of the actual site. Another and perhaps more widespread factor is that when a soil becomes acid it tends to form raw humus, a layer of purely organic material on the surface. If left undisturbed such a layer behaves very much like peat and can be subjected to pollen analysis in the same way, as was Iversen's site in Denmark, where the raw humus reached a depth of over 70 cm.[83] Usually it is much less than this because raw humus, which can become very dry in the summer, is susceptible to fire. Wherever man has been active he has used fire, and one result will have been the repeated destruction of the raw humus, so creating a gap in the pollen sequence. Sometimes we can detect a raw humus beneath the peat, and pollen analyses may show a sharp difference between the humus and the underlying mineral soil, an indication of the lapse of an unknown stretch of time between the two pollen records.

One effect of a peat layer is to prevent the deposit of later pollen on any archaeological level buried beneath it, but the same result can be achieved by burial under other covers. Earthworks of many kinds may preserve prehistoric soils beneath them, and in such soils pollen of the prehistoric period may be preserved if the acidity is great enough[170] (Dimbleby, 1962). Not only may such soils yield evidence of the contemporary vegetation, but from the profile pattern it may be possible to trace the changes which have preceded the construction of the earthwork. Raw humus layers can and do occur in this context too, thereby complicating the time scale. Nevertheless, the pollen spectrum contemporary with the construction of the earthwork can often tell us what the landscape was like at the time – whether it was wooded, whether clearings had been made, and if so, whether pastoral or arable agriculture was being practised. However, even in apparently suitable soil conditions special circumstances can sometimes militate against satisfactory results. For instance, the buried soil may have had its upper layers removed, having been truncated by erosion or by deliberate paring, so that the layer containing the contemporary pollen is missing (Dimbleby, 1962, pp. 61–6). Sometimes such a lack is offset because the earthwork is made up of turves cut locally and these yield pollen. In some cases they show varied pollen spectra indicating different places of origin, perhaps from different parts of the clearing in which the site was set. Another source of trouble is contamination of the buried soil by pollen from the overlying earthwork. Fortunately pollen is slow-moving in

soils and movement is only significant in the upper metre or so. Consequently any earthwork which stands higher than that should be safe, and
indeed satisfactory results have been obtained from even slighter ones.[164]

Old land surfaces may be buried by the mass movement of soil material,
such as wind-blow or hillwash. This may be of natural occurrence, for
instance in coastal dunes or in mountainous regions, but elsewhere it is
often attributable indirectly to human activity. Pollen analysis has shown
that many of our soils are complicated by the addition or removal of
material at some period of instability, and this often seems to have coin-
cided with phases of forest clearance.[34] Whether or not the land surface so
covered had archaeological remains on it, the fact of such an erosional
phase apparently linked to human activity should be of concern to the
archaeologist.

Caves offer special problems to the pollen analyst. It is difficult to tell –
and we have virtually no data to guide us – to what extent the atmosphere
in a cave becomes infused with pollen from outside. It is likely that such an
influence will be mainly in the cave mouth and pollen-rich sediments may
be effectively sealed by occupation débris and roof-falls. Caves are commonly in limestone and their floors are therefore likely to be calcareous,
a condition which as we have seen does not favour pollen preservation.
Nevertheless, in caves in the Alps pollen has been found,[9] and it is clear
that much more research is required into the palynology of such sites. They
may offer special problems of interpretation even if pollen profiles can be
established: just as the vegetation round a rabbit burrow can be drastically
modified as compared with the surrounding field, so the vegetation near
the entrance to a cave may have been profoundly affected by fire, nitrogenous refuse and other factors. As the pollen in the cave entrance would
reflect the nearest vegetation most strongly, data are urgently needed on
this point.

Coprolites (fossil faeces) are a special source of pollen which may have a
close connection with caves in arid areas. As we have seen, they can
contribute both environmental and dietary information.[108]

Apart altogether from its environmental significance, pollen analysis can
provide interesting facts about the actual structure of earthworks. It has
already been mentioned that turves included in constructional works can
show different pollen spectra, indicating different sources of origin. In the
same way the mineral soil making up an earthwork can also be shown to be
heterogeneous and sometimes it is apparent that the material did not come
from the immediate vicinity at all (Dimbleby, 1962, pp. 53–6). Pollen

analysis can also help to answer another question that frequently arises in excavations: did the material of which the mound (or rampart) is built come from a ditch or was it scraped up from the surrounding soil? In many cases the question can be answered on other grounds – colour, texture, and so on – but this is not always possible. In a normal soil the upper layers are pollen-rich, but the quantity of pollen falls off with depth until at about 50 or 60 cm it is negligible. Consequently, a mound made up of topsoil scraped up from the surrounding area will be rich in pollen throughout (Dimbleby, 1962, pp. 49–53), whereas one constructed from a ditch will mostly be poor in pollen.[158] Both forms have been demonstrated in Bronze Age round barrows. This same change in the abundances of pollen with depth also enables us to say whether the turves of a turf-mound are upright or inverted; this is not always apparent visually, and in fact both arrangements can occur, even in the same mound.

The applications have so far only been made to sites in cool-temperate conditions, where they are obviously most likely to be profitable. It would be rash to prejudge the usefulness of pollen analysis in other circumstances. The possibility that pollen may be preserved deserves serious investigation. It has recently been established that pollen can be present in sun-dried mud-brick; some samples of this material from the early neolithic site of Çatal Hüyük in Turkey were quite rich in pollen, others were devoid of it. Such research could lead to important archaeological as well as environmental conclusions, though there are considerable difficulties in interpreting analyses of this sort.

Nothing has yet been said in this chapter about the significance of spores. Spores are microscopic bodies released by most non-flowering plants in order to disperse the species. Many are airborne and they are commonly found in pollen preparations.[61] Spores are seldom identifiable to the extent that pollen grains are, though in certain cases they have proved to be of considerable significance. For instance, a special type of spore, the teleutospore, is produced by rust fungi, and the teleutospore of the rust of wheat, *Puccinia graminis*, was discovered in quantity in a coffin in the Great Barrow at Bishop's Waltham.[5] From this it was inferred that the coffin was lined with wheat straw to receive the cremation. Generally fungal spores are not identified, though one feels that with some of the more complex ones recognition should be possible. Here, however, one comes up against the problem of reference material for comparison; the fungi are very numerous and very diverse, and their systematy is no matter for the layman. Some moss spores are recognizable, more particularly those which grow in peaty conditions and are therefore looked for in the deposits. The *Sphagnum* mosses in particular have spores which can be identified – though not usually down to species – but the spore production of mosses is a much less regular affair than the flowering of the higher plants, so the records have less significance.

By far the most abundant spores encountered in pollen analysis are the fern spores. Many of them are indistinguishable, being kidney-shaped with no other strong features apart from size differences. There are exceptions: the spores of common polypody (*Polypodium vulgare*) are unmistakable, and the same is true of bracken spores. The latter is a plant which reacts vigorously to human influence so that we are fortunate that its spores are recognizable. Less important (from the archaeological viewpoint) are the royal fern (*Osmunda regalis*), moonwort (*Botrychium lunaria*) and the adder's tongue fern (*Ophioglossum vulgatum*), whose spores are also identifiable. These are British species but in other parts of the world there are other ferns with distinctive spore types. The club-mosses (various species of *Lycopodium* and *Selaginella*) also have spores which can be recognized, even to species, and as these plants have strong ecological affinities, their occurrence is of environmental importance.

The spores of ferns and club-mosses are generally extremely resistant to decay. Consequently they may be the last remaining types in a medium which is biologically active. When a peat bog undergoes a phase of drying out, for instance, the bulk of the pollen may be destroyed and practically nothing but fern spores is left. It must be recognized, however, that not all pollen types are equally resistant to decay. There are many species whose pollen we seldom or never find, even though we know them to have been present. This applies more to the herbs than to the trees, though in the latter category mention should be made of poplars. The difficulty may partly be one of recognition, but there seems little doubt that the pollen of some species is evanescent. It is fortunately true that the pollen of most of the important ecological dominants is resistant to decay: most trees and shrubs, the grasses and the heath family (Ericaceae). Even so, there are degrees of resistance, so that the more decomposed the material is the more over-represented certain species will tend to be. The pollen of lime (*Tilia*) is a good example.

In the compass of a book of this sort it is not possible to give detailed guidance on sampling for pollen analysis. Circumstances vary, materials vary and the questions to be answered vary. The sampling pattern must be arranged in such a way that the results can be interpreted in the manner desired. Ideally sampling should be done by the pollen analyst himself, for, apart from anything else, he will find it very useful when interpreting his analyses to have a first-hand knowledge of the site. This, however, is often not possible. If the excavator himself is taking the sample, the following simple points should be borne in mind. First, the samples need only be of small size – about a matchboxful; if it is too big it may cover several pollen horizons and interpretation becomes meaningless. Secondly, contamination must be avoided. The chief sources of this are pollen (and also pollen-rich dust) in the atmosphere and the material of the section itself. Sampling must therefore always be from a newly-cleaned face, with a clean sampling tool of whatever type is being used, and precautions must be taken against material falling into the sample from the section. Series of samples, when taken, should therefore be taken from the lowest levels first, leaving the highest – and usually most pollen-rich – layers till last. Once taken each sample should be sealed immediately. The third point is to reduce as far as possible any decay in the sample before it reaches the pollen analyst. Here we should recall those factors which prevent pollen decay – waterlogging, drought and cold. The latter is seldom of any practical use until the samples reach the laboratory, when they can be stored in a refrigerator until they can be dealt with. For samples from waterlogged sites it is desirable to keep them waterlogged; it usually suffices to seal them in a tube or plastic bag leaving as little air space as possible. With non-waterlogged samples it is best to dry them. Air-drying is normally sufficient, though oven-drying at about $105°$ C is safer if it can be done. It is sometimes said that drying spoils the pollen grains and makes recognition more difficult (Faegri and Iversen, 1975), though personally I have never found this a difficulty. But it must be appreciated that mineral samples have probably undergone many vicissitudes of wetting and drying before the samples were taken; this may account for the fact that the state of the pollen is in any case much worse in such samples than in those from waterlogged deposits. If air-drying is adopted, this should be done without exposing the samples to the atmospheric pollen rain or they will become contaminated. Some pollen analysts add a drop or two of toluol or a little phenol to their samples as preservatives, but it is safer not to rely on these alone if there is going to be an appreciable delay in the samples reaching the laboratory.

Finally, a practical point which is not always apparent to the excavator: if you are working outside Europe or North America pollen analysis may be possible in theory but not in practice because no botanist has yet worked on the pollen of that region. This situation is rapidly becoming rarer, but it still exists. Sometimes illustrations in the form of drawings or photomicrographs are available[46, 47] and these can be of great assistance, but by themselves they are not enough. They must be backed by a reference collection of the pollen grains themselves. Without adequate reference material pollen analysis can even be misleading rather than helpful, and should not be undertaken.

Other plant remains

Apart from wood, which has already been considered, many other plant parts have been found in prehistoric or archaeological contexts. It is difficult here to distinguish between archaeological sites proper and the many sites of environmental importance (e.g. peat bogs) which, though providing no direct contact with archaeology nevertheless may have significant implications for it. Equally, there are many cases of vegetation analysis from the prehistoric period which have no apparent link with man. The fossil plant record will obviously be much more complete from a waterlogged peaty site than from a terrestrial occupation site, though the latter may have more carbonized remains. In general, the parts of plants which we come across and which can be made to tell a useful story are much the same whatever the situation; differences come in the degree of preservation. For our present purpose, therefore, we will not discriminate too minutely between archaeological and other palaeo-botanical sources.

By far the most informative plant remains falling under our present heading are seeds and fruits. From wood it is seldom possible to take identification beyond the genus, and with pollen, too, it is rarely possible to get as far as species. Fruits and seeds, on the other hand, can usually be taken to species under good conditions of preservation. Carbonization always brings about shrinkage, to a degree partly dependent on the way the process is carried out, so in cases where size or proportional dimensions are critical there may be difficulties. Nevertheless, as reference to the works of Helbaek,[75] van Zeist,[184] Hopf[77] and others will show, even with this sort of material the majority of seeds and fruits found in archaeological sites can be identified to species.

It is not possible in the compass of this book to give a comprehensive picture of the range of seeds and fruits even for Western Europe.[17] The variation is enormous. Fruits may be huge, like the vegetable marrow, pumpkin, melon or gourd (all cultivated members of the family Cucurbitaceae), containing many seeds, or they may be small enough to be airborne and contain only one seed (e.g. many Compositae). Seeds themselves vary enormously too; some are as fine as dust, such as some orchids, whilst at the other end of the scale is the familiar horse chestnut. Tropical trees can show even larger seeds. Seeds and fruits may be dispersed in various ways, and this determines their shape and special features to a large extent. Fruits or seeds which are dispersed by wind have wings or a parachute of hairs (pappus) and these features alone provide many variations. Others are dispersed by attaching themselves to animals; these have hooked spines or, in the case of many grasses (including the cereals), bristle-like awns with reversed teeth along them. Yet others have edible fruits and are dispersed by being eaten by animals or birds, the resistant seed being voided later perhaps many miles away; such fruits are usually fleshy, and naturally are of direct interest to man as an article of diet. There are many other devices – pepperpot mechanisms, explosive fruits, protective shells (nuts), and so on – all related to the perpetuation of the next generation. But having said this it must be added that there is also a great deal of variation which seems to have little relation to function, but which is nevertheless of great assistance in identification. Unfortunately there is no comprehensive work in the English language dealing with European species, but a number of books give illustrations of a limited selection; examples are Godwin's *History of the British Flora* (1975) and Salisbury's *Weeds and Aliens* (1964).

Reference was made above to Helbaek's work in the archaeological field. His material has been of three main types: carbonized fruits and seeds, impressions accidentally fired in ancient pottery, and, less commonly but of comparable importance, the stomach contents of the corpses in bog burials.

Helbaek[72] removed the alimentary tract from the Tollund and Grauballe corpses, and washed out the contents from the stomachs and intestines. Though the plant material in them was finely divided, presumably having been ground in food preparation and then masticated, it was possible to recognize the smaller intact seeds, and the fragments of larger seeds and associated plant parts. The preservation was remarkable; even starch and albuminoid matter apparently had preserved their structural and chemical properties unaltered, though one might have expected such substances to have been hydrolysed. Helbaek listed over sixty species of cereals, wild grasses and other plants, most of which today we would regard as weeds. Some of these weeds, such as corn spurrey (*Spergula arvensis*), Gold of

Pleasure (*Camelina sativa*) or persicaria (*Polygonum persicaria*) were so abundant that they may have been cultivated in their own right.

It appears that these bog corpses were killed in mid-winter (for discussion see Glob[53]), and Helbaek comments that the species found were all seeds or fruits that could be stored. Most of the species concerned had already been identified in Denmark in the Iron Age or earlier, but nowhere before had such a rich collection been found in one place. This assemblage gives rise to theories about the normal diet of Iron Age people (Glob[53]), for the last meals of these two men were notably deficient in animal matter, but Helbaek argues that a ritual sacrifice, which is what these corpses seem to represent, may have involved a ritual meal, and that this mixture, probably prepared as a gruel, cannot be taken as typical of the everyday diet of the people. However, it is possible that some of these plants, which today we regard as weeds, were cultivated for their own sakes.

A point that Helbaek does not mention is that some of the species found are generally regarded as poisonous to man. Some of these, such as knotgrass (*Polygonum aviculare*) and yellow rattle (*Rhinanthus minor*), are only recorded as traces. Black nightshade (*Solanum nigrum*) was rather more frequent in the Grauballe man, though this is a plant whose poisonous properties vary widely in different localities (see [52, 117]). The buttercups are also toxic, but here the toxic agent is present in the sap and breaks down on storage, so it may be that seeds ingested in mid-winter would be harmless. We can conclude, therefore, that the health of these two men was not so likely to be affected by what they ate as by what happened to them an hour or two later.

Reference was made in Chapters 5 and 9 to fungal diseases of crops and the possibility that evidence of these might be detected in preserved material. In these bog corpses Helbaek found profuse evidence of plant disease, including ergot (*Claviceps*) sclerotia and spores of various smuts (*Ustilago* spp.). In many cases these disease organisms were attacking wild grasses and some of the weeds, but direct evidence was found of barley disease brought about by a fungus of the Dematiaceae, a family which includes a number of seed-borne parasites of cereals of economic importance, and also by the covered barley smut, *Ustilago hordei*. It is important when material of this sort is found that it should be drawn to the attention of specialists such as plant and animal pathologists. This is what Helbaek did, with impressive results.

Through this approach Helbaek has added a great deal to our knowledge of the history of agricultural crops and of the weeds associated with them,[70] and in particular his work on the cultivated cereals[69] has given us direct evidence of which cereals were first cultivated and where. From both carbonized grain and from pottery impressions, he has been able to recognize the primitive wheats einkorn, emmer, spelt, and later the bread wheats. It is also possible to distinguish the other cereals, barley, rye and oats. From the material extracted from sites in the Near East Helbaek has been able to trace the development of a tough rachis (central stalk) to the ear, a desirable development if the grain is not to be scattered during harvesting, and the appearance of naked grains in wheat and barley, that is grains which separate easily from the enclosing glumes. These trends have already been referred to in Chapter 6, and it is to this approach to seed analysis that we owe the facts on which the morphological side of the evidence is based. Complementary to this there is the work of the geneticists and the plant breeders.

Carbonized seeds have bulked largely in the palaeo-botanical evidence derived from prehistoric sites in North America, and here too it is found, as shown in Chapter 2, that 'weeds' apparently formed major items of diet. In Central America, the hunt for the origins of maize[106] has hinged almost entirely on the morphology of the cobs found in archaeological settings, the cobs being virtually the only part of the maize plant to be preserved, presumably because they were the only part collected and brought to the domestic site where they might become preserved.

As with wood, in which the cell structure is preserved perfectly on carbonizing, so with fruits and seeds there is often an astonishing degree of detail preserved. Even fleshy fruits are sometimes preserved, complete with carbonized flesh; I have seen a prehistoric cherry preserved in this way. The cell structure of the hazel-nut shell is virtually unchanged by charring; hazel nuts are one of the commonest wild fruits in archaeological sites, being found in large quantities as far back as the Mesolithic. Their abundance indicates that they were undoubtedly an article of diet. This is also indicated by the fact that almost invariably they are broken when found in archaeological sites, though in other contexts they may be entire. In the last decade there has been something of a revolution in the extraction of fruits and seeds from archaeological deposits. This has been brought about by the development of flotation apparatus in which fine air bubbles are passed through a tank of liquid as the deposit samples are poured into it.[85, 133] The seeds and other organic materials come to the surface and are decanted through a series of sieves. Less sophisticated and easily constructed forms of flotation apparatus have also been used with success on archaeological deposits.[118] Until such techniques were used the presence of seeds was often not even suspected; now the amount of material extracted is sometimes so large that the archaeologist hesitates to burden his botanical colleagues with the very time-consuming job of identifying it. It is important, therefore, that the archaeologist should have clear reasons for taking such samples.

Before we leave the subject of fruits and seeds, no doubt it will be expected that something should be said about mummy wheat and the claims that some of it is still viable. All that needs saying, however, is that these claims have not stood up to critical examination.[13] Some seeds can apparently retain their viability for a century or two when stored, for instance in museums.[55] Even when lying in the soil dormancies of decades are not unusual, and of centuries are apparently possible (Salisbury, 1964). But these Methuselahs of the seed world are usually seeds with extremely hard seed-coats, so that it is necessary to treat the coat mechanically or chemically before it can germinate. Wheat grains are not protected in this way, and indeed, as Helbaek[75] points out, the extreme desiccation by which mummy wheat is preserved is also the agency which would kill it.

Grasses have a tendency to build up silica into their leaves and stems, as well as into the fruits and this is probably responsible for the very clear-cut impressions sometimes obtained, for example, on pottery or in tufa casts. Furthermore, when a grass leaf or the bract-like glumes and paleas of the flower spikes are burnt to ash, this silica persists and the cell structure of the epidermal tissues, even including hairs and stomata, can be preserved in exquisite detail. These skeletons are, of course, extremely fragile, but Helbaek[75] has found them preserved in pottery, which has protected them, and he has also recovered recognizable fragments from ash heaps in the Near East. Besides this preservation of the leaf cells themselves in mineral form, however, the grasses frequently contain silicious bodies known as phytoliths or plant opal.[151] These are laid down in certain cells in the epidermis and they vary considerably in shape and in their dimensions. Unfortunately it cannot be said that the shapes are consistent enough to enable grasses to be identified as far as species from them, but at least some grouping of species seems possible.[110] In spite of this lack of precision, the recognition of phytoliths is significant as proof of the presence of gramineous material in the particular context; in this respect it differs from pollen which could be wind-carried to a greater or lesser degree. Silicification of tissues is not confined to the grasses, though it is best exemplified in them. Characteristic phytoliths also occur in sedges (Cyperaceae), but there is little coherent information on other types of plant, though, as we have seen, the presence of silica in wood elements has been established by wood technologists.[24] It should be remembered that one would not find silicious remains in preparations of soil in which treatment with hydrofluoric acid had been used, as this acid dissolves silica. This means that preparations of mineral soil for pollen analysis will not contain them if this acid has been used.

Microscope slides prepared for pollen analysis frequently contain other leaf fragments whose nature is apparent, though at the moment they are only useful for identification in particular cases. For instance, pieces of epidermis may be found containing not only normal epidermal cells, which themselves can have various and distinctive shapes, but also stomata, the pores of the leaf. Stomata are formed by two guard-cells and sometimes other subsidiary cells, and may have various complications of structure which can give them characteristic appearances. In raw humus derived from pines the stomata may remain recognizable long after all other microscopic structure of the leaf has disappeared, sometimes after the pines themselves have gone. I have found pine stomata at least 100 years old, and there is no apparent reason why they should not be preserved in fossilized soil organic horizons. If they are found their significance, as with phytoliths and silica skeletons, would be that the litter of the species had actually decayed on that site; usually this would mean that in all probability the species was growing there. A similar argument has centred on the occurrence of tracheids of ferns, particularly bracken, in prehistoric sites on the chalk.[41] In this case the stomatic remains seem likely to have been derived from the mucking out of cattle bedding.

Under good conditions of preservation whole leaves – sometimes whole plants – may be preserved. This may sometimes be seen for instance under round barrows, especially on wet acid soils. Even under these conditions identification may not be easy; a black, squashed and distorted herb can look very different from the living plant. Nevertheless, even if preservation is not as complete, recognition is sometimes possible where highly characteristic features persist. Leaf fragments, especially if they include a part of the leaf margin, may be identifiable, and even sub-microscopic features like leaf-hairs can be complex in structure and therefore likely to be recognizable. Godwin (1975) illustrates leaf-hairs of mullein (*Verbas-*

cum) and sea buckthorn (*Hippophäe*), which have been identified from Late-glacial deposits.

Bud-scales are a specialized form of leaf and these have been identified in the fossil state in German work;[130] though bud-scale analysis has not been applied extensively to archaeological sites, it has been shown that they may be found under good conditions of preservation.[8] The presence of resins and other water-repelling materials in bud-scales may contribute to their preservation.

Plant material derived from stems (excluding wood, which has already been dealt with) appears in the archaeological record in a number of forms. Occasionally lengths of stem, perhaps with leaves attached, may be found. Fragments of grass stems and leaves are particularly worth submitting to a field botanist for identification because a great deal of attention has been directed by agricultural botanists and ecologists to identifying grasses in the vegetative (non-flowering) condition. Much depends on how much is preserved and how well, but it is worth a try. Usually one needs a length of stem and a leaf arising from it complete with ligules (if present) at the junction of leaf and stem. In some cases the lower part of the stem is a necessary feature. Remarkable detail of grass stems is sometimes preserved in casts in pottery or in tufa, but these are of limited value because even if the cast includes a node it is not possible to study features such as the ligule or the hairiness of the leaf or stem.

Among the charred remains of wood one not infrequently finds pieces of charred bark and these are usually submitted along with the charcoal by the archaeologist. In fact, with the naked eye charred bark is not easy to distinguish from charred wood, but under the lens or microscope the difference is immediately apparent. Unfortunately bark lacks the detailed tissue structure which makes wood identification possible, so that it is virtually useless for identification. When large pieces of bark occur it may be recognizable on macroscopic features; for instance the characteristic platey structure of pine bark or the corky bark of field maple (*Acer campestre*) is usually recognizable even by the layman. The specialist, however, is not able to take matters very much further than the layman in less clear-cut cases, and will have to turn to supporting evidence of a different sort, such as wood or pollen.

Perhaps the most important stem material (apart from wood) from the archaeological point of view is fibre; and what is said about stem fibres applies equally to leaf fibres. Wood fibres, which are an essential element in the xylem of the stem, have already been described in that context; being closely bonded with the other woody tissues they cannot easily be separated out and so are of little utilitarian value. Other fibres, however, occur in the tissues outside the wood, notably in association with the pericycle or phloem – the conducting tissue mainly concerned with the transport of synthesized food reserves (Fig. 3). Like the wood fibres, bast fibres play no part in the conductive processes but are purely mechanical. In some plants these fibres occur as sheets or strands running with the phloem, and in other plants they may be insignificant or even lacking. Where they do occur they are relatively easily separated because they are a tough, usually lignified, tissue surrounded by soft unstrengthened cells. Frequently the stems were retted, that is left to soak in water until bacterial decay has disorganized the soft tissues, making extraction of the fibres easier and cleaner. This is still standard practice in the linen industry.[96]

Like wood fibres, bast fibres are long dead cells with pointed ends – not square-ended, as they have been described in at least one text-book. The walls are very thick, leaving only a very narrow lumen and they may be lignified and even impregnated with silica. It has been said that bast fibres from different plants are almost indistinguishable; but it is in fact possible to identify the most important species. There are great variations in length and thickness[96] – lengths of individual fibres range from over 400 mm in ramie (*Boehmeria*) to a fraction of a millimetre. Flax fibres have nodes, which sets them apart from other fibres used by early man. Though perhaps not strictly within our subject, it is interesting to note that cotton fibres are recognizable by being twisted, but of course they are different in nature from bast fibres. This whole subject of vegetable fibres in an archaeological context calls for more research.

The use of the 'cambium' as a source of food was mentioned in Chapter 2. To be botanically correct cambium is not the proper term; as we have already seen 'cambium' itself is a girdle only one cell thick which is in an actively meristematic (dividing) condition, producing wood cells on the inside and phloem cells on the outside (Fig. 3). The nutritious part of the 'bark' is really the phloem, its value arising from the fact, just noted, that it carries the new food reserves manufactured by the plant. The phloem is relatively most abundant in the young shoots; as the stem increases in girth the radial thickness of the phloem is proportionally reduced. In elm, the tree so much sought after, the phloem contains mucilage cells, in addition to the parenchyma, sieve-tubes, companion cells and ray cells, all of which are living and therefore rich in nutrients. The mucilage cells are most abundant in the phloem of the young shoot and they serve to provide that agglutination which is necessary for the making of bread from such material. The name slippery elm, the easily digested invalid food made from a certain species of elm, is a direct reference to this mucilaginous content; indeed it has been suggested that the word 'elm' itself means slimy or slippery. However, these highly nitrogenous and nutrient-rich materials are just as palatable to the micro-organisms of decay as they are to man, so it is not surprising that archaeological records so far have not revealed this usage. Indeed, one of the factors which makes such material palatable to man is the absence of tannins, substances which if present might have delayed decay.

Other parts of plants occasionally show up in archaeological contexts, though rarely, considering the uses to which they were put by primitive man. Charred tubers (not identified) have been found in prehistoric sites in North America. Flax plants with roots attached have been recovered from the Swiss pile-dwellings and these have enabled Helbaek[72] to deduce that this was the winter-annual race of flax (Winterlein), a form which is still grown in the mountainous region of Southern Germany.

It was shown in Part I that non-flowering plants also contribute to man's needs, but it is relatively rarely that they are recovered from archaeological sites.[143, 171, 178, 179] Mosses are, perhaps, an exception especially those with tough stems which allow them to be used as fibres. In this field, too, there is scope for further research, especially in the direction of plant diseases. Traces of fungal infections have been found on plant tissue of prehistoric age from non-archaeological sites and there seems every likelihood that a careful examination of the better preserved plant remains would produce similar results from archaeological sites. These might have ecological, climatic or even cultural significance, particularly if they affect staple agricultural crops.

Finally, we should mention here resins and allied substances – perhaps not plant remains in the strict sense, but derived from plants, and, as we have seen, being very useful to early man. Apart from the dry conditions which have preserved such things in, for example, Ancient Egypt, one occasionally comes across such material among charcoal. It is difficult to say whether it is in fact charred resin or wood tar but it is characterized by a clean, polished fracture, the surface of which often shows flow patterns. Such occurrences are no doubt accidental in the majority of cases, but it may be expected that deliberately collected resin may occasionally become preserved in this way.

Part 3

Interpretation of the evidence

11

The man-made landscape

In the second part of this book we have considered the conditions in which the remains of plants, or of artefacts made from plants, may be preserved. Moreover, we have seen to what extent actual identification of this material may be possible, giving the archaeologist a sometimes surprising amount of detail about what uses man was making of plants and what those plants were. Observations of this sort, however, are of value far beyond the immediate archaeological application. Archaeological sites offer direct evidence of the occurrence of certain plants at a certain date, and as we have seen from the discussion of pollen analysis they can offer information which is not obtainable by other methods of enquiry into the past, such as peat analyses. They therefore complement such other sources of information; indeed in some geographical regions they may be the only source. If this is true for plant material it is even more true for animal remains, which include no parallel in distribution and persistence to that remarkable phenomenon, the pollen grain. Here, too, enquiry has been much too anthropocentric. A good deal has been made of remains of vertebrate skeletons because of their obvious direct connections with man, but the insects, for example, have been neglected, despite the fact that their chitinous exoskeletons are relatively resistant to decay. Archaeology has much to offer to the biological sciences, a fact which the scientists themselves have been slow to appreciate; and it could be said that this even applies in some degree to the physical sciences.

In this chapter we shall look at the contribution of archaeology in giving us an understanding of the changes in the landscape which have taken place during man's long history, and try to assess the degree to which he himself has been responsible for this. It will be necessary to concentrate largely – but not exclusively – on one region, so I have selected north-western Europe as being an area for which a good deal of information exists and the area in which my own experience has been centred. In making this survey we are not leaving archaeological considerations aside; in the first chapter it was argued that one of the most important aspects of plant life to early man was as the background in which he lived and which gave him shelter and fertile land. In that chapter we looked at the concept of vegetational climax and noted the possible consequences of disturbing that climax. Some of these consequences will form the subject of the next chapter, but here our concern is with the changing pattern of vegetation.

It is important to realize that from the earliest time – when the name man was first befitting – man has had at his disposal great power for changing the nature of his surroundings. In particular he had fire. Time and time again, when evidence of fire is found in the course of excavation – reddened stones, charcoal, cracked flints – the question is asked by archaeologists: is this due to natural fire or to man-made fire? One must always allow that natural fires do occur; in some circumstances, such as coniferous forest or in climates with a long dry season, they may be frequent. In temperate forests, however, they are rare – unless the forest has already been opened up so that a fire hazard has developed; for example, a ground cover of bracken. One must also ask whether a natural fire, which is often quick-travelling, could produce the effects observed; would it redden large stones right to the centre? This is not the place to discuss this subject fully; it will simply be assumed that if man is known to have been present, fire is far more likely to have been due to him than to natural causes, especially where the vegetation (e.g. coniferous forest or savanna) is susceptible to fire.

It has been customary to assume that before man introduced agriculture he lived in his environment but had no effect on it. That this should be so when we know that he possessed fire was put down to the fact that the population was so small and scattered that even if he did start a fire it would be on a very local scale. But, once started, fires are not as easily contained as that, and it is significant that the vegetational record is now beginning to show the sort of evidence that one would expect. This has come about through the refinements in the techniques of pollen analysis, in particular the increased attention devoted to the non-arboreal pollen, which quickly reflects any disturbance of the tree cover. Rarely do circumstances allow us to detect the influence of palaeolithic man, but such a case seems to have been revealed by West[173] from the Interglacial deposits at Hoxne. Here the pollen sequence showed a marked drop in tree pollen accompanied by a corresponding rise in grasses and other light-demanding species. At the same level charcoal occurred, and Acheulian flint tools were tied in to the same horizon. Views differ as to whether man caused the fire, or merely exploited the effects of a natural fire, but it is curious that there is only this one episode in the whole of the Hoxnian sequence.

Coming to the Post-glacial period, considerably more evidence is now building up, both from pollen diagrams and from mesolithic sites themselves. The effect varies from case to case; most commonly there is an increase in grass pollen and associated herbs, as at Hoxne, but bracken can also show a similar response, or even trees such as birch and hazel. On very acid soil heather has been found to attain dominance on mesolithic sites. Such effects have now been demonstrated in Britain from the Pennines,[63] Dartmoor,[144] the Kennet valley[183] and the southern heaths.[93] In France, too, similar patterns of clearance have been recognized, and it has been pointed out that mesolithic man had added another powerful ecological weapon to his armoury – the grazing animal. Remains of domesticated sheep, goat and cattle are now known from a number of pre-neolithic sites in Western Europe,[135] and when we turn to the Near East – the cradle of agriculture – we find evidence for the same precession of domestication. Grazing and browsing are just as destructive of forest as fire, and if maintained can lead to widespread deforestation. However, they usually go hand-in-hand, fire creating conditions favourable to grasses and shrubs, which in turn are fed upon by animals. It has been suggested with good reason that before domestication even wild animals profited from the effects of fire in producing and maintaining grassland and that palaeolithic man in turn depended upon this relationship.[137, 145] This could well have been the case, for instance, in the North American Plains, but in Western Europe, under a more oceanic climate, forest was probably a much more vigorous invader, and the fire risk would be correspondingly less.

We are not able yet to estimate the extent of these early inroads into the all-covering forest. As the peat sequences usually reveal these events as only minor changes in the pollen-rain, it appears that they were essentially local. Such evidence from the peat bogs, however, may not distinguish between a number of very small clearances, such as might be made around temporary camp sites, and one relatively bigger one as might result from an uncontrolled fire. The actual archaeological sites themselves may eventually give us some idea of how extensive the clearance is round one site, but it will not tell us how many similar sites existed at any one time.

It also has to be borne in mind that mesolithic man was present in Britain through the earlier millennia of the Post-glacial period, a time when warmth-loving plants, and especially forest trees, were reaching Britain from the Continent. Recent evidence suggests that regular burning by mesolithic man may actually have prevented the establishment of forest above 350 m altitude in the Pennines, where one would have expected it to have constituted the climatic climax.[84]

Even in these remote periods botanical investigation can sometimes cast interesting sidelight on human activity. The site at Oakhanger, dated on charcoal to around 5600 B.C., is a case in point.[132] This site lies on very acid sands, yet among the charcoal found there was wild clematis (*Clematis vitalba*), a species which is confined to calcareous soils. It had presumably been brought from the chalk country, several miles away, because of its usefulness as rope or cordage. In the same site there was also a high concentration of ivy (*Hedera*) pollen, still in a mesolithic context but not necessarily coeval with the charcoal. Ivy is an insect-pollinated plant whose pollen normally appears as only a trace, but in one sample here it reached 87% of the total count. Troels-Smith[163] has suggested that evergreen plants were used as winter fodder for stock, and this could be the explanation here. Ivy is unusual in flowering from September to November, so if the plant were being collected for winter fodder it would be in flower and the pollen would become concentrated on the site. A very similar concentration of ivy pollen has also been recorded at several other sites of mesolithic age on one or two occasions from the Bronze Age.[158] Its occurrence at Oakhanger, however, may be seen as indirect confirmation of mesolithic husbandry, perhaps involving the red deer in particular. By the way, the widespread impression that ivy is poisonous to animals is not true, though sheep and deer are apparently more partial to it than are cattle. Other evergreen species which have been used as winter feed are mistletoe (*Viscum album*), of which sheep are particularly fond, and holly, with which sheep and deer can cope much better than can cattle (Johnson, 1867).

When we come to the agricultural periods much more definite evidence of change in the landscape is forthcoming. Even so, the evidence is still somewhat piecemeal; one fact which complicates the picture is that the neolithic settlement was largely concentrated on the better (base-rich) soils – which do not preserve pollen well – and generally shunned the acid soils. These were utilized in the Bronze Age. However, we can learn something of neolithic clearance from Denmark, where acid soils were cleared, perhaps because there was less choice of land type. Here pollen analysis has revealed progressive waves of land clearance, each followed by the regrowth of the forest.[90] It is interesting to observe that this regrowth became progressively more difficult as time went on, presumably due to gradual deterioration of the soil. In this country, too, it has shown how in the Bronze and Iron Ages similar temporary clearances occurred in the landscape surrounding peat bogs;[166] sometimes there were many such clearances (not necessarily all in the same place) before total deforestation occurred. Furthermore, though we refer to the forest, we cannot assume that it was always the same forest as far as its botanical composition was concerned. One of the features of the breaking up of the original forest continuum has been that it has been accompanied by a progressive change in the floristic composition; the originally rather varied tree flora becomes simplified, with oak becoming relatively more dominant as other species drop out.[37]

When this general clearance occurred – which it did at varying times in different places – it is possible to tell what was being done in that area. Where the opening up of the forest results in greater representation not only of grass pollen but also of the pollen of the Compositae (especially *Artemisia*, the mugwort or wormwood), Ranunculaceae, *Rumex* (sorrel and docks), Chenopodiaceae and Caryophyllaceae, we may be reasonably sure that arable cultivation was being practised. Sometimes this is confirmed by the occurrence of cereal pollen grains, though the absence of these is not conclusive. Most cereals are self-pollinated, the flowering spikelet never fully opening, so pollen is not released in large quantities into the atmosphere. Occasionally, however, the presence of cereals may be established by the finding of a small cluster of cereal pollen grains adhering together, having presumably come from an undehisced anther or an unopened flower spikelet.[95] In this condition wind transport is likely to have been negligible, so it can be deduced that the cereal was probably present on that site. A word of warning should be given about the identification of cereal pollen grains, which are like wild grass pollen only much larger. There are some wild grasses which also have grains large enough to make for confusion, and careful examination is needed before cereal pollen can be recognized with absolute certainty; this may necessitate the use of sophisticated apparatus such as the scanning electron microscope. Where seed or grain impressions can be recognized on pottery, of course, we then have proof positive of arable cultivation, but the pottery cannot tell us exactly where the cultivation was taking place.

In many cases forest clearance is not accompanied by the array of weeds listed above; there is merely an increase in grass or heather pollen, perhaps with bracken spores showing a parallel trend. Here clearance may have been accidental or deliberate, and if the latter, was probably done to favour pastoralism. In Britain this was usually the case over 300 m in altitude.[36]

A word should be said here about an incidental, but for man very important, side effect of clearance: namely the great stimulus which it gives to the growth of shrubs. Hazel, for instance, though an understorey component of the high forest, does not achieve the vigour of growth and the abundance of flower and fruit which it does in the open. The impression is gained from pollen analyses (proof is virtually impossible) of a zone of hazel scrub between the undisturbed high forest and the open clearing. Hazel pollen is found in large quantities even in soils which are now covered by moorland (a line of thought which will be developed in the next chapter); it seems to have been almost ubiquitous. Sometimes alder reacted similarly, and on the chalk, judging from the charcoal finds, blackthorn (*Prunus spinosa*) and hawthorn (*Crataegus* sp.*), seem to have behaved in much the same way. It must also be remembered that these shrubs may also form the pioneer woodland phase when land was abandoned – no doubt a far more frequent occurrence then than now. There is good evidence that they – and a number of others – played no small part in prehistoric economy from the Mesolithic onwards. Hazel nuts are found in quantity on some sites, where they were clearly used for food; carbonized sloes have been found in sites on the chalk. The shrubs would also offer, in an easily accessible form, raw materials such as poles, bark and fibre, but not so apparent would be their value as browse for stock. Hazel is very palatable to herbivorous animals, and when growing as thicket it is often in association with a grass cover. It is interesting to note that hazel can still be found in some of the woodland inclosures in the New Forest, but only in those that are adequately fenced against stock. The thorns are less likely to be eradicated by grazing, but even they can suffer badly; the young shoots may be eaten before they have developed their full armoury.

Botanical studies of buried soils beneath earthworks can shed interesting and sometimes puzzling light upon the siting of these structures. Certainly the impression is gained that Bronze Age round barrows are frequently sited on land which had been abandoned because of weediness or, on acid

* Hawthorn wood is indistinguishable from apple or pear, but in view of the quantity found it seems the most likely species in this context.

soils, because of the spread of heather (Dimbleby, 1962); this is under-
standable. Not so easy to digest is the fact that some Iron Age hill-forts
were built in dense oak forest; two or three cases are known in Britain –
not many perhaps, but then not many have been investigated in this way
(Dimbleby, 1962, pp. 76–8). Combination of the botanical evidence with
the characteristics of the buried soils in many cases gives valuable data on
ecological trends which, of course, involve the soil no less than the vegetation itself. Even the pollen analysis of the present surface soil of an earthwork can give valuable information on the vegetation history since the
earthwork was built. This may or may not be of archaeological significance,
but it can be of great ecological importance in the understanding of the
present status of the landscape. It sometimes happens that an earthwork
has been enlarged from time to time, so that it contains a series of old
surfaces within it. Round barrows which have been enlarged after secondary burials may have three surfaces: the buried soil, the surface of the
mound before it was extended, and finally the present surface of the
mound.[36] From the botanical study of such a series the progressive
changes in the landscape may be revealed. A special case of this type of
study was provided by some circular banks of unknown purpose on
Studland Heath, Dorset.[40] Here it turned out that one bank had been
raised four times, and the pollen sequence indicates the progressive re-
treat of hazel scrub and the replacement of grassland by heathland, a
process apparently covering several hundred years, perhaps a millennium.

It is not common for one monument to give much scope for comparative
studies. Much greater possibilities are offered where a number of earthworks of different ages occur in the same area. The size of the area appropriate for such study depends on its ecological uniformity; many square
miles may be acceptable in some cases, only a few acres in others. What is
to be avoided if this approach is used is the comparing of data from monuments of different ages in widely different ecological contexts. Where
conditions are (or better, were) reasonably uniform it is possible to
establish a sequence of change of vegetation, and once this has been done it
has even proved possible to assign undated monuments to their appropriate
period on the basis of the condition of the landscape at the time they
were built.[33] An interesting example of this comparative method is the
study of the buried surfaces beneath monuments of neolithic, Bronze
Age and Iron Age date on one small area of moorland near Great Ayton in
Yorkshire. The modern soil surface gives a fourth period, and from the

four, as Fig. 5 shows, it is possible to trace the deforestation of the area, and the development of agriculture; perhaps most interesting is the evidence that the landscape only became heather-clad moorland, its present state, after the Iron Age. Certainly four rough time fixes in a period of 4–5,000 years are not a very satisfactory sampling pattern, but this ecological sequence, crude though it is, could not have been established in any other way.

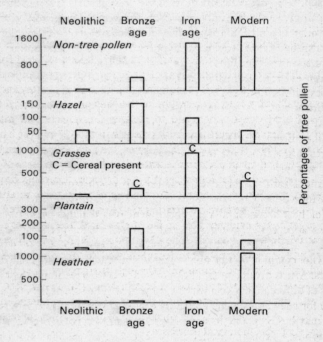

Pollen analyses of buried surfaces
Great Ayton Moor, Yorks. N.R.

5. Comparative pollen analyses showing deforestation, spread of agriculture and subsequent development of moorland.

The archaeologist should be aware of the type of landscape in which the subjects of his study were living. This is certainly more widely realized now than it was fifty years ago, when the means for elucidating past vegetation were not available to the extent that they are now. It was a puzzle then to imagine mesolithic man living on the hills covered in nothing but heather,[44] which as far as was then known was the case. Now we know that these hills carried deciduous woodland in mesolithic times – a totally different environment not only from the point of view of shelter but especially as a habitat for game, a main staple of life. The vast reed-swamps of the Nile Valley, which were the source of the papyrus which was of such varied use to the Ancient Egyptians, were gradually converted into agricultural land by drainage schemes, until now it is difficult to appreciate their former extent. This principle is of general importance, the more so where the ecological conditions were marginal so that the hand of man brought about very great changes. The archaeologist can be forgiven for finding it difficult, standing in a treeless tract of moorland, to imagine that a mere 5,000 years ago it was oak forest; or, working on a site covered by the blown sand of the desert, to imagine the place well grassed, perhaps even wooded. Incontrovertible botanical evidence is necessary to make such flights of imagination credible, but it is often present, though rarely sought, in the sites themselves.

12

The damaged soil

The reason for including a chapter on soils in a book on archaeological botany is simply that the plant remains found in archaeological sites enable conclusions to be reached about the condition of the soil and the influence which early land use (or misuse) had on it. Other forms of evidence, of a non-botanical nature, also contribute to our understanding of soil changes, but at the risk of making an artificial distinction these must be excluded here.

In the first chapter of this book it was shown how the vegetative cover of the earth protected the soil against the extremes of the physical factors of the environment, and that in due course of time some form of equilibrium – or at any rate relative stability – was usually achieved between the climax community of living organisms and their physico-chemical environment. Man's problem has always been – whether he realized it or not – to modify this equilibrium for his own purposes without allowing undue scope to the forces of denudation against which the vegetation was giving protection. As one might imagine, his efforts have been largely trial and error; reasoned control of land use is a very modern concept, and still quite a rarity.

Consider the succession expressed in the following general terms:

Open water———>reedswamp———>swamp woodland———>mesic forest (climax).

This represents a progressive decrease in the wetness of the habitat, culminating in the mesic (that is, medium) moisture condition in the climax forest. Destruction of this climax condition, or even the modification of it, must make conditions relatively wetter, since the control exercised by the climax forest will have been weakened. It can be demonstrated that the destruction of woodland derived in this way leads to a higher water-table. More commonly, however, the climax is the culmination of a succession in which water is progressively more efficiently conserved; e.g. as follows:

Bare ground———>grasses———>dry woodland———>mesic forest
(climax).

Here the result of interference will be the opposite of the case just quoted; the habitat will become progressively drier. There are, of course, many intermediates between these two extremes of hydrologic sequences, but perhaps enough has been said to make it clear that it is not necessarily true, as has been said, that destruction of forest cover *always* results in drier conditions. It must be allowed, however, that wherever there is a dry season – and this applies to vast tracts of the earth – the overall effect will be of desiccation. Furthermore, man has made some of his greatest strides towards dominance of his environment in just such climates. In such conditions the equilibrium between vegetation and environment tends to be precarious, especially during the dry season, so that a minimum of disturbance may have a disproportionately large effect.

The archaeological evidence of site deterioration in places with a marked dry season is often very considerable, but relatively rarely is it based on the plant remains, so it falls outside our present scope. Nevertheless, there may be botanical indications that in earlier conditions moisture was more available (apart from climatic change); crops and weeds, indicated by charred remains and perhaps pottery impressions, could only have grown under better hydrologic conditions than pertain now. In those cases where irrigation was used salinization was not uncommonly the result, and this might be reflected in the vegetation, particularly by the spread of plants of the Chenopodiaceae. The occurrence of pollen of this family in mudbrick may have a number of explanations, but salinization could be one. Another effect of increased aridity may be erosion, but we will leave this until later in the chapter when it will be considered as the outcome of several forms of degradation.

Increased wetness may also be indicated by factors other than plant remains; the development of a soil characteristic of wet conditions, such as a peaty gley, for instance. But botanical evidence is often present too. There may be remains of vegetation which can be identified as characteristic of wet conditions. Remains of cotton-grass (*Eriophorum* sp.), for instance, have been found on the soil surface buried beneath a Bronze Age round barrow, and the pollen analyses may show the increase of the pollen of Cyperaceae (sedges), the family to which this plant belongs. Other species characteristic of such a change in water conditions and which show up in pollen analyses are the devil's-bit scabious (*Succisa pratensis*) and tormentil; at the same time there is nearly always a decrease in the representation of herbs which like drier conditions, such as plantains (*Plantago* spp.) and members of the Ranunculaceae.

Changes in wetness or dryness are not the only ones brought about by disturbance of the forest. In temperate regions changes in acidity are often more important than changes in the hydrology; soils developed on a parent material poor in lime – and these are widespread in northern regions of both Eurasia and America – are particularly prone to such a change. In these soils there is at equilibrium a precarious balance between the loss of mineral nutrients (especially the bases lime and magnesia) and their replacement by weathering of the soil parent material; or they may be brought on to the site in the water supply. One of the effects of de-forestation is to kill the deep roots of the trees on which the extraction of these substances from the deeper layers of the soil depends. As a result the soil becomes more acid and this apparently can happen quite quickly – a matter perhaps of a few decades. The ramifications of this change are profound and are widely reflected in the botanical evidence from pre-historic sites. For one thing, a soil which was not acid enough to preserve pollen may soon become so, and the pollen record tells us what the vegetation was like when this stage was reached. In Britain it was usually in the open hazel scrub stage intermediate between forest and open coun-try. The process was also aggravated by practically everything that primi-tive man did. Fire provides an ash dressing to the soil which may be of initial benefit to the crops, but which is readily soluble so that on a light sandy soil part of the nutrient capital is lost through drainage. Cropping of both plants and animals also inevitably removes quantities of these same substances from the site. The effect is most marked in the surface layers of the soil but becomes progressively deeper.

In order to show the full implications of this process in the reading of the evidence of changes brought about in the landscape by man, it is necessary to take the story a little further. It may appear that the details become rather non-botanical, but it must be remembered that the sequence has been pieced together very largely from the pollen analysis of soils and surfaces buried beneath earthworks (Dimbleby, 1962).

Let us assume that the soil under the original forest was a brown forest soil, carrying an active earthworm population. One of the effects of acidification would be to eliminate the earthworms that are responsible for soil mixing, as they are intolerant of acidity. Many bacteria, too, would go the same way. As a result the surface of the soil would change, losing any crumb structure it had, becoming less porous, and developing a covering of acid raw humus. As the acidity increased there would be a replacement of some of the original species of grasses and herbs by others more tolerant of acidity, whose effect is very often to make the humus even more acid – a vicious circle. In due course visible bleaching of the upper (A) soil horizons would occur as the iron, together with other more important substances, was leached out and deposited in an accumulation (B) horizon at a lower depth – the early stages of podzolization. The raw humus which develops on such a soil is at one and the same time the strength and the weakness of the system; it gives protection to the now structureless soil beneath, but it is also vulnerable to fire and if burnt off leaves this soil in danger of erosion by wind or water. All these stages have been clearly demonstrated on archaeological sites, and the pollen sequence not infrequently shows that wind erosion or hillwash has followed close on the heels of forest clearance, even as far back as mesolithic times. This is indicated by the occurrence deep in the soil of a layer with all the characteristics of a pollen-rich soil surface, over which perhaps a foot-depth of sand or gravel has been deposited.[34, 93, 132] On upland sites in the north of England mineral layers washed into peat bogs have been dated to the Mesolithic, clearly indicating erosion by water at this time.[146]

The degradation of the soil surface can, however, have far-reaching effects of a different nature on soils of heavier texture and where the rainfall is higher. Again the key is loss of structure but the result now is to cause impedance at the surface by the colloidal absorption and resultant expansion of the base of the raw humus layer. This, it has been suggested, is the cause of thin iron-pan soil formation (though not, I believe, the only cause), with reducing conditions developing below the humus layer and causing the mobility of the iron in the ferrous state. However that may be, there is frequently a change in the vegetation to a wetter facies, and I think this could be the first step to peat formation. In fact, all stages between wet raw humus layers and deep hill peat can be found in upland areas.

Does this mean that the growth of hill peat is due to man rather than to climate? Yes and no. There are many places, particularly where water collects, where the peat growth may be directly related to climate; this is a straightforward topographical, not a pedological, condition. Nevertheless, there has been a tendency to extrapolate ecological sequences from this type of situation to the very different circumstances in which hill peat occurs. It is true that bog growth demonstrably killed oak forest in the Fens of East Anglia, for instance.[56] But this is a hydrologic collecting area, and it does not follow that forest growth on, say, the Pennines, was killed in the same way. There are certainly cases where high-level bogs have burst or flowed downhill and engulfed forest, but this cannot be the explanation for the replacement of forest by bog on vast tracts of our uplands. Forest is a vegetation type well suited to high rainfall. Rain forests are known under a wide range of climates. I myself have seen forests on the Pacific Coast of North America, at the latitude of Brittany, on acid glacial till, with a rainfall of over 3,500 mm per year; there was a raw humus layer 2–6 cm thick and no trace of peat formation. Moreover the bleached horizon also was scarcely 5 cm thick. Why, then, have we got hill-peat instead of forest? I believe we would still have had forest if there had not been repeated destruction by fire and grazing from mesolithic times onwards. Recent work by Moore[112, 113] shows that there is consistent evidence of man's influence in pollen analyses from the base of our blanket peats.

In this discussion so far I have deliberately left out any reference to climatic change. Archaeologists are not alone in a tendency to invoke climatic change to explain what after all is no more than a change in microclimate as far as our evidence usually goes, so for once we have left climatic change till after we have looked at other aspects. There is good evidence for climatic change (see also the next chapter) and it must have had some effect – even an over-riding effect in some places. The evidence from archaeological sites shows that changes in vegetation of the type we have been discussing have happened at any time from the Mesolithic – perhaps even the Palaeolithic – to the historical period; the same can be said about the various forms of soil degradation. We can expect that climatic change would have had an effect in places like basin sites, as we have already seen, but on normal free-draining land surfaces the evidence seems to suggest that the initial major changes in vegetation type were due to man and not climate. This is not to say that climate did not alter the floristic composition of the vegetation, but not to the extent of altering its ecological character.

Nevertheless, there are widespread changes which did apparently occur in association with a climatic change. The deterioration of climate at the beginning of the Iron Age is substantiated by evidence from a variety of sources, and being the most recent of the major Post-glacial climatic changes, the effects of it are still detectable. Mention has already been made of the widespread growth of hill peat and blanket bog; another instance is the spread of heather to form many of our present heathlands and moorlands. (It must be said, however, that in some places, e.g. Dorset,[141] the heaths are apparently of much earlier origin.) Increased soil erosion has sometimes been attributed to the increased rainfall, as has the growth of peat in basin or estuarine sites. But all these things, and others not mentioned here, are probably not primary changes, but are consequent upon the previous occupation of the habitat by man. It has already been shown how this could lead to peat formation; the spread of heather is a likely event on soils already acidified, and it would be favoured by a climatic change which told adversely against arable farming on acid soils, especially in the north. Erosion, too, is unlikely to be purely due to climate, but will take place where the soil has been exposed. Land use, therefore, appears to be a *sine qua non* of the environmental changes referred to, and this makes any deductions about the effects of climatic change *per se* highly questionable in areas where man has been active. This conclusion does not apply only to north-temperate conditions but is fundamental to all regions.

As a corollary to this, it must be apparent from what has been said that changes can take place in the habitat which are of a similar nature to those brought about by climatic change, but which in fact occurred purely and simply through man's action under constant climatic conditions. Increased soil desiccation, perhaps even leading to the onset of desert conditions, is a widespread example which is still going on. In fact erosion of one sort or another is one of the commonest environmental changes of which the archaeologist finds evidence, and it is very often taken as indication of climatic change. Even association with climate, it appears, is more beset with difficulties than we realized, for recent work in the northwestern United States suggests that whereas major erosion had been thought to take place in a dry climate, it now appears that it was due to a period of intense summer rainfall.[107] In oceanic climates such as that of Western Europe such a state is less likely. Nevertheless, as far back as 1927 Erdtman[45] described several bog profiles from north-east Yorkshire in which mineral soil had spread over the bog surface from the edge, in one case to a depth of 75 cm. The pollen showed that this material was deposited during the Sub-atlantic period, and Erdtman took it to mean much-increased precipitation. All one can really say, however, is that runoff was increased, and this could have been due to deforestation of the surrounding catchment area. More recently, Godwin and Vishnu-

Mittre[59] have demonstrated similar accumulations in peat in the Fenland and have attributed them to the effects of agriculture in the Bronze Age, about 1400 B.C. Many soil profiles I have examined by pollen analysis have shown that they have acquired new material by wind-blow or hillwash, and time and again this can be matched up with a period of forest clearance;[34] as we have already seen, this process has been recorded on a number of archaeological sites of mesolithic age.

Erosion is frequently brought about by increased run-off and this must have repercussions in basin sites such as the examples just mentioned, or in estuaries. The increased influx of both the water and the silt it carried must bring about changes in the hydrologic conditions of such areas. This may have its repercussions on human life in such places. For instance, wooden trackways across boggy or marshy areas have been set in their environmental context by pollen analysis of the peats upon which they lie and by which they are now buried.[54] From these it is sometimes concluded that these tracks represented an attempt to keep communications open in an area which was becoming increasingly swampy. Whether increasing wetness was due to climatic change, however, cannot be said with certainty until a complete study has been made of the hydrology of the catchment and its collecting areas. Obviously an increase in rainfall would have this effect, but it is not the only factor concerned.

It is not possible to give a comprehensive account of the damage which man has done to his environment – and continues to do – without drawing upon non-botanical evidence as well, which is beyond the scope of this work. However, the botanical evidence alone is enough to show that from earliest times man has modified his environment and laid the land open to the ravages of those factors of denudation against which the vegetation was giving it protection. It has been tacitly assumed in these pages that the climax vegetation is pretty well constant in any one period of climate, though ecologists do not all agree on this point. It is therefore appropriate to end this chapter by considering briefly one theory which suggests that there is a progressive decline of the status of the climax – the theory of retrogressive succession. This is a matter of some importance to archaeology because some of the changes which are suggested are almost indistinguishable from those brought about by man; moreover, one of the proponents of this theory was the late Professor J. Iversen, the Danish botanist, to whom, as we have already seen, archaeology owes so much.

Before looking at some of Iversen's evidence, however, let us turn first to the work initiated and stimulated by the late Professor Pearsall in the

Lake District of north-west England[119, 120] and so ably carried on by Dr W. Pennington. By studying the cores brought up from the beds of lakes it has been possible to trace certain trends. Chemical and physical analyses, together with pollen analysis, have shown how in the early stages of the Post-glacial the lakes received a great deal of mineral detritus from the unconsolidated land surface and its immature soils in the vicinity of the lake. As time went on and forest clothed the landscape this input was reduced and for a long time a slow and steady accumulation took place. But at about 3000 B.C. things began to change; evidence began to appear of increased soil acidity and there was an acceleration of the inflow of mineral detritus, implying a greater erosion. At the same time the pollen indicated a certain amount of forest clearance and its partial replacement by grass and other light-demanding vegetation. Clearly this represented a new rate of ecological change from the slow one that had gone before. This new rate of change continued for 3,000 years or so and there was a further speeding up of acidification and erosion into the lakes. At about 3000 B.C. the neolithic impact was being felt in the Lake District – and the pollen analyses give abundant evidence that it had a direct effect on the vegetation. Between 1000 B.C. and Roman times there was apparently a progressive increase in the population resident in the hills. Then it seems to have dwindled, but whether due to the rival attractions of Roman settlements (as Pearsall suggested) or to the increased erosion of the hillsides indicated by the lake analyses, cannot be said. The question remains – has man created new conditions and instituted new processes in the environment, or has he merely speeded up a process which was inevitable?

This is where we must introduce Iversen's evidence, from Draved,[83] a piece of woodland which had apparently escaped disturbance right up to the present day. There had been one brief episode of fire but the effect was apparently transitory. The reason for this almost unique state of affairs seems simply to have been that this wood grew on rather poor and undesirable soil, and was by-passed by the age-old migration routes into Denmark from the south. Here still persisting was the prehistoric type of forest we have talked about, with not only oak but also alder and even lime persisting on the better soils. The great depth of humus on the forest floor, up to 70 cm, was analysed for pollen by Iversen, showing that it dated back for 3–4,000 years. This long run of time gave an unparalleled opportunity for tracing back the history of one tract of forest for thousands of years. Iversen's results showed a gradual change in the composition of the forest as time went on. Trees which are regarded as characteristic of richer soils, such as alder, lime and ash, gave way to those better suited to poorer or more acid soils; oak became more predominant and birch increased in importance. Moreover, Iversen showed that on the poorer tracts of soil in this forest, where soil deterioration would be more rapid, the rate of change in the floristic composition was correspondingly quicker. He therefore concluded that in the undisturbed state there was a tendency for the ecological system to run down, for the soil to become more acid and less fertile, and that this retrogressive succession, as he called it, was least conspicuous upon the more base-rich soils (with mild and not raw humus).

Does this trend come to a steady state or does it continue indefinitely perhaps to the point where forest can no longer survive? At the moment we cannot answer this question but alongside it we may set another question that French ecologists have been asking about the status of heathland derived from oak forest after the initial forest clearance in the Neolithic. Can this heathland, they ask, ever become forest again, or has it now reached a new climax state at a much lower level of organization? They conclude that it could never revert to forest and describe its new state as paraclimax.[43] However, I have worked on equivalent areas in Britain and I am firmly of the opinion that they can revert to woodland;[32] indeed, given complete protection from fire, and assuming seed is available, the process can be surprisingly rapid.

I raise these problems here because they do, I think, provide part of the answer to the questions arising from Iversen's and Pearsall's work. Iversen has demonstrated retrogressive succession, but against this must be set the fact of progressive succession, such as the succession from heathland to forest. It may be that the two actually come together in a common woodland climax. I am convinced that under undisturbed conditions Iversen's retrogressive succession will not lead to deforestation (and all that that implies for the soil), because it is quite apparent that under equally undisturbed conditions, forest is established by normal succession from grassland or heath. Applying this to Pearsall's question for the Lake District, it seems that we must answer in two parts: (a) there may be a certain degree of retrogressive succession leading to a change of forest type, and the influence of man may be to promote this change; (b) but where this change goes beyond the forest state to a simpler type such as heath or grassland, this is a man-made condition which nature will remedy if the anthropogenic factor is removed.

From the work of Pearsall and his co-workers (particularly Mackereth [103]) it is apparent that soil erosion in one form or another becomes progressively more pronounced as deforestation proceeds. This no doubt applies with less force to the richer soils where a grassland sward is little inferior to forest in preventing soil erosion, but we are brought back nonetheless to the point from which we started – that when man started clearing forest he also set in train some powerful adverse soil factors. Archaeologists would do well to bear this in mind whenever they get the opportunity to study man's impact on his environment.

13

Plants and chronology

It is probably true to say that most archaeologists, if they pay any attention at all to plant remains, do so in the hope of obtaining a date from them. If this subject is left till the last chapter of this book, and then dealt with rather briefly, it is not because I regard chronology as of subsidiary importance, but only because the subject is already well covered in the literature.[186] Moreover, it is a subject on which plants, whilst making an important contribution, are by no means the only sources of dating material, so that a full treatment cannot be given here in any case. However, the contributions which plants have to make are interesting because of the very diverse ways in which they can be made to tell a chronological story.

RADIOCARBON DATING

This well-established technique,[11, 21, 180] still less than three decades old, depends upon the basic physiological process of the life of the green plant, the conversion of carbon dioxide from the atmosphere into plant tissue and food which is stored in the plant. When the plant tissue dies it contains in effect a sample of the carbon dioxide of the contemporary atmosphere. At any time the atmospheric carbon dioxide contains a very small proportion of radioactive carbon which becomes incorporated in the plant tissue and then proceeds to decay. On the assumption that the proportion of radioactive carbon in the atmosphere remains constant (an assumption which is not absolutely true, but which we cannot discuss further in this context), if the amount of residual radioactive carbon can be measured and if its rate of decay is accurately known (another assumption which has given some trouble), it is theoretically possible to estimate how long ago the tissue was formed, so that if the plant material can be associated with human culture, that culture can thereby be dated. I have avoided referring to the age of the plant, preferring the term plant tissue.

This is to cover the fact that in a long-lived species the date at which the plant died may be very different from that at which the oldest tissue was laid down. For example, in a giant redwood the heartwood cells may have been laid down 2–3,000 years ago and have long been dead, though the tree – as a plant – is still alive. In long-lived trees, therefore, it is important to know where the sample which was used for the radiocarbon estimation originated, and this cannot always be established with accuracy.

It is not my intention here to expand on the potential errors in the measurement of the amount of radioactive carbon, nor upon the time-scale over which the method can safely be applied. These considerations are the subject of much technical research and debate; most people concerned with radiocarbon dating, whether they be the physicists or the users of the results, are perfectionists, and the recognition and elimination of potential errors are permanently under investigation. Perhaps we are too prone to demand more and more without stopping to think what has really been given to us in the last 25 years or so. To compare our uncertain chronology then with the remarkable framework we have now is to see a near miracle; no less remarkable is the achievement of the physicists in making this possible on such very small amounts of the radioactive isotope.

From the botanical standpoint a few words may usefully be said about the nature of samples most suitable for radiocarbon dating. One of the main dangers is contamination by organic matter of a different (usually later) period, which is very liable to occur if the sample has been buried in soil, as most archaeological samples have. Charcoal is the most suitable material because it is composed of elemental carbon which resists violent chemical treatment; it is therefore possible to destroy infiltrated humus and other organic matter without destroying the charcoal itself. The more humified other materials are, such as uncarbonized wood, the less easy it is to separate the humified substance of the sample from secondary humus. Peat is something of an exception here; reliable radiocarbon dates have been obtained and matched with pollen analyses from the same levels.[60] This is presumably due to the fact that peat is stratified and virtually inert with little water-movement – which would transport humic materials – from layer to layer. For the same reason objects buried in peat may also give reliable dates, even though they are not in an ideal condition. A highly humified piece of wood, perhaps an artefact, could be a source of a reliable date if buried in peat, but it would have been much less useful had it been derived from a site on a freely-drained soil.

Plant material is not, of course, the only source of radiocarbon dates. Animals which have fed on vegetation – perhaps at second or third hand – may also be used in this way. It would be desirable to know how long – in years – the food chain was between the animal and the green plant food on which ultimately it depends, though this is not likely to be a serious source of error. Animal tissues may also contain carbon which is derived from the mineral environment, from the calcium bicarbonate of wells and water supplies; this is concentrated in the hard skeleton, for instance, of molluscan shells, and for this reason radiocarbon dating of shell or bone is done on the included collagen and not on the mineral skeleton.

TREE RING DATING

Most people living in temperate latitudes will be familiar with the fact that in cross-section tree trunks show more or less well-marked annual growth ring. These are caused by the rapid production of relatively thin-walled wood cells during the early part of the summer growing season, followed by slower growth in the later summer, the cells becoming smaller and more heavily thickened. After the winter dormancy the new growth the following spring makes a clear contrast with the old. This is essentially a result of rhythmic growth and does not occur where there are no seasonal differences in growth rate. It is for this reason that we have no direct means of telling the age of some of the giants of the tropical rain forests; they have no growth rings. In fact radiocarbon dating has actually been used to estimate the age of the huge bulbous-stemmed baobab (*Adansonia*); it turned out that there was an age difference of about 1,000 years between heartwood and the bark.[157]

However, certain species of trees in which growth rings do occur live for very much longer than this and provide a valuable record of changes in growth rate over a long period of time: 2–3,000 years for the redwoods (*Sequoia sempervirens*) and big-trees (*Sequoiadendron giganteum*) and over 4,000 years for the bristle-cone pine (*Pinus longaeva*), an insignificant and gnarled tree which grows extremely slowly in the semi-desert region of Arizona. The important feature of these living records is not so much the length but that they contain distinct patterns of narrow and wider rings which are not accidental but are a direct reflection of changes in the environment.[10] In the semi-arid regions of the United States it is variations in climate which produce these differences – broad rings associated with moister years and narrow ones with years of exceptional drought – and the same ring pattern will therefore be found in all the trees of one species living over the same period of time. The patterns of rings in living trees may be linked by overlap with the patterns shown in dead timber, and by this method of linking up (or cross-dating) it has been possible to obtain a run of over 6,000 years in the Western United States. The principle becomes archaeologically significant when timbers used in the construction of ancient buildings can be fitted into the known sequence, as was done by Douglass[42] using the western yellow pine (*Pinus ponderosa*) which, being the typical tree of the dry regions occupied by the Pueblo Indians, was used by them for constructional timber. It thus was possible to date many Indian sites, though even with this straightforward method of dating there are inherent sources of error. For instance, old timbers may be reused in new buildings; and where trimmed timber is used the outer rings – the important ones for dating – may be missing.

Apart from this direct application to archaeological dating, however, tree ring analysis is important to archaeology in two other indirect ways. One of the most important developments in chronology has been the use of tree rings, which give an absolute date, as a check on radiocarbon dating. From cores from the bristle-cone pine 10-year ring samples of exactly known date have had their radiocarbon age determined; by this means it has been possible to calibrate the radiocarbon technique.[156] It transpires that the radiocarbon date curve is not truly linear, which accounts for some of the anomalies of radiocarbon dating which had worried archaeologists concerned with ancient civilizations where independent means of dating were available.

Secondly, on the assumption that tree rings are controlled by climate, their pattern is seen as a record of past climatic change, a record which could be matched with pollen analyses and other indicators of climatic change. Indeed, it has been suggested that these climatic changes in their turn determine the behaviour and way of life of human population.

However that may be, it needs to be said that the occurrence of a pattern in a tree-ring sequence is in itself no proof of direct climatic relationship. The rings as we see them in cross-section are merely reflections of differences in growth rates, and there are many factors which can influence growth rates. The defoliation of a tree by insect parasites; differences in soil texture and drainage; severe late frosts; these are some of the factors, apart from rainfall, which can modify the ring pattern. In fact in some parts of the world, especially where the climate is not extreme, there are so many sources of ring pattern other than climate, that tree-ring correlations, if possible at all, have to be interpreted with extreme care. The real value of the method comes in those places where there is a strongly adverse season so that growth is restricted. Any alleviation of this condition will lead to the more rapid laying down of wood, and unduly harsh conditions to its virtual cessation. The conditions in the south-western United States, where the method has been used so successfully, were just of this nature, with a long dry summer, the growing season, when fluctuations in rainfall assumed major significance for the trees. Even so, it is recognized that errors can occur even under these conditions; sometimes two rings appearing in one year, sometimes none at all.

Tree-ring sequences have now been found to be valid in quite different climatic settings. In Europe sequences based on beech and oak are in use, and in Britain oak has been used to complete a sequence covering the period from the late prehistoric to the medieval.

Relatively little work has been done on the parallel use of different species in tree ring work. It is possible that species of different ecological requirements might react in different ways to changes of climate and so augment the information which could be obtained from only one species. On the other hand, some species are notoriously unreliable in the laying down of rings; birch, for instance, is very prone to produce false rings, that is, rings in addition to those which are due to the normal seasonal pattern. Such false rings may not completely encircle the stem, but if one is working with cores and not complete sections this would not be obvious.

POLLEN ANALYSIS

We have already seen that pollen analysis depends upon the remarkable resistance to decay which is a feature of many pollen grains. Reference to Fig. 6 will show at a glance the principles upon which dating by pollen analysis is based. From the end of the glacial period the climate became progressively warmer, tundra and grassland phases being replaced by woodland of birch, pine and hazel, and these in their turn giving way to the mixed oak forest (including particularly alder, oak, elm, lime, as well as hazel) of the Atlantic period – the culmination of temperature improvement since the last ice extension. The Atlantic period came to an end about 5,000 years ago, since when the effects of climatic change have become confused with the effects of man's influence on the vegetation. As we

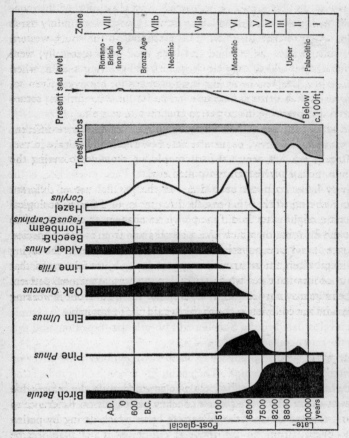

6. Simplified diagram of the pollen sequences in the Late- and Post-glacial period Britain. By permission of The Linnean Society of London (after West, *Proc. Linn. Soc. London*, vol. 172, 1961).

saw in the last chapter, even the climatic deterioration at the end of the Sub-boreal period is blurred in this way. For instance, is the spread of birch a response to a reversion of the climate, is it due to the progressive opening up of the forest, or to a progressive leaching of the soil, or do all factors apply? However, it is not necessary to answer these questions in order to recognize the distinction between the Sub-boreal and Sub-atlantic, and on such bases pollen analysts are able to divide the Post-glacial period up into pollen zones, characterized by different assemblages of pollen types, the trees being the most significant. There is no universally-agreed system of zone numbering, or even of the number which is recognized. In Britain we use eight, in Ireland ten, and nine in Denmark. Features which are important in one region may be insignificant in another. If an archaeological level, or an artefact, could be reliably related to a certain tree pollen spectrum, then it should be possible to match this spectrum to one of the recognized pollen zones. This, in essence, is the principle of dating by pollen analysis.

It should be noted that this so-called dating is not in fact absolute; it only becomes a dating method if the pollen zones themselves can be given a chronology by tying them in with a method such as radiocarbon dating. This in fact has now been done for many areas. However, even then there are considerable limitations to the accuracy of dating by pollen analysis, for a pollen zone may have persisted for over 2,000 years. Sometimes one can detect the influence of two zones, as for instance when lime is present along with beech in buried levels in Southern Britain; it is reasonable to assume that the level is dated to the Sub-boreal/Sub-atlantic transition, and this narrows the range considerably.

A little while ago the influence of man was mentioned, the effect on birch being taken as an example. The possibility is now having to be faced that some other plants critical in pollen zonation may also have had their distribution affected by man. The elm decline has widely been recognized as marking the end of the Atlantic period, but evidence is accumulating that elm suffered from the initial forest clearance in the Neolithic.[121] Earlier in this book we have seen how elm was useful to early man for wood, fibre, bark, cattle fodder and even food for himself. Troels-Smith[163] makes an interesting deduction from the elm-wood 'funnel-necked beaker' (see p. 46) found in a Danish bog. The wood was in fact bird's-eye elm, a figure in the wood which is caused by the repeated cutting back of the tree. If the tree were repeatedly lopped for cattle fodder in early neolithic times it would produce just such a figure in the wood. Elm has been referred to as the 'poor man's tree', an indication of its many uses;[116] it is hardly surprising that its distribution was affected. But elm is also a calcicolous tree (that is, favouring base-rich soils), and its further decline, which continued until its virtual disappearance at the end of the Bronze Age, may have been caused in part by progressive soil acidification, itself the result of man's activity. Wych elm, the species most likely to be involved in oceanic Europe, is still a vigorous species on calcareous soils, so we may doubt whether its falling away after the climatic altithermal (the Atlantic period) was in fact the result of a cooling of the climate.

Another species which behaved in much the same way as elm was lime (*Tilia*). Again we have no conclusive evidence that on climatic grounds alone it would have been eliminated, for its decline is compounded with the clearance of forest for agriculture.[165] However, like elm, it was an extremely useful tree to early man and a very acceptable fodder for his stock, and Iversen[82] has shown that in Denmark it disappeared from the forest early where initial forest clearance was early, later where it was later, and as we have seen he found it still present today in the wood of Draved which had escaped clearance altogether.

Though these considerations may weaken the reliability of pollen dating, particularly in the second half of the Post-glacial, they emphasize the fact that the occurrence of species and communities is a matter of ecology, and ecology embraces other factors than climate. Pollen analysis has played an enormous part in the elucidation of vegetative and climatic changes through the Post-glacial (and earlier), and even if it is now taking second place to radiocarbon as a method of dating it still has a vast amount to tell us on questions of ecology and land use, as we have seen. In some ways it is a good thing for archaeology that it should no longer be thought of as merely a dating method, for it opens the way to much wider applications.

General References

Ashby, M. (1969) *Introduction to Plant Ecology*. (2nd edn.), London.
Biek, L. (1963) *Archaeology and the Microscope*. London.
Butzer, K. W. (1971) *Environment and Archeology*. Chicago.
Childe, V. G. (1957) *The Dawn of European Civilization*. (6th edn.), London.
Clapham, A. R., Tutin, T. G., and Warburg, E. F. (1962) *Flora of the British Isles*. (2nd edn.), London.
Clark, J. G. D. (1952) *Prehistoric Europe : The Economic Basis*. London.
Cornwall, I. W. (1964) *The World of Ancient Man*. London.
Darlington, C. D. (1973) *Chromosome Botany and the Origins of Cultivated Plants*. (3rd edn.), London.
Dimbleby, G. W. (1962) *The Development of British Heathlands and their Soils*. Oxford.
Driver, H. E. (1964) *Indians of North America*. Chicago.
Faegri, K., and Iversen, J. (1975) *Textbook of Pollen Analysis*. (3rd edn.), Oxford.
Forest Products Research Bulletin No. 22 (1959) *Identification of Softwoods by their Microscopic Structure*. London.
Godwin, Sir H. (1975) *History of the British Flora*. (2nd edn.), Cambridge.
Hodges, H. (1964) *Artifacts*. London.
Jane, F. W. (1970) *The Structure of Wood*. (2nd edn.), London.
Johnson, C. P. (1867) *The Useful Plants of Great Britain*. London.
Lucas, A. (1962) *Ancient Egyptian Materials and Industries*. (4th edn.), London.
Moldenke, H. N., and Moldenke, A. L. (1952) *Plants of the Bible*. New York.
Paulssen, L. M. (1964) *Identification of Active Charcoals and Wood Charcoals*. Trondheim.
Piggott, S. (1965) *Ancient Europe*. Edinburgh.
Renfrew, J. M. (1973) *Palaeoethnobotany*. London.
Salisbury, Sir E. (1964) *Weeds and Aliens*. (2nd edn.), London.
Sauer, C. O. (1952) *Agricultural Origins and Dispersals*. New York.
Tschumi, O. (1949) *Urgeschichte der Schweiz*. Frauenfeld, Switzerland.
Ucko, P. J., and Dimbleby, G. W. (Editors) (1969) *The Domestication and Exploitation of Plants and Animals*. London.
Yarnell, R. A. (1964) 'Aboriginal Relationships between Culture and Plant Life in the Upper Great Lakes Region.' *Univ. Michigan Anthrop. Papers*, No. 23.

Detailed References

1. ANON (1858) 'Account of the Ancient Canoe found at Burpham, near the River Avon.' *Sussex archaeol. Collections* 10: 147–50.
2. ANON (1961) 'An Atlas of End-Grain Photomicrographs for the Identification of Hardwoods.' *Forest Prod. Res. Bull.* No. 26. London.
3. ALEXANDER, J. (1973) 'The domestication of yams; a multidisciplinary approach.' In: *Science in Archaeology* (Editors, D. Brothwell and E. Higgs). (2nd edn.), London: 229–34.
4. ALEXANDER, J., and COURSEY, D. G. (1969) 'The origins of yam cultivation.' In: *The domestication and exploitation of plants and animals* (Editors, P. J. Ucko and G. W. Dimbleby), London: 405–25.
5. ASHBEE, P. (1957) 'The Great Barrow at Bishop's Waltham, Hampshire.' *Proc. prehist. Soc.* 23: 137–66.
6. ASHBEE, P. (1958) 'Excavation of a Round Barrow on Chick's Hill, East Stoke Parish, Dorset.' *Proc. Dorset nat. Hist. and archaeol. Soc.* 80: 146–59.
7. ASHBEE, P. (1963) 'The Wilsford Shaft.' *Antiquity* 37: 116–20.
8. ATTWATER, C. (1972) *The identification of bud scales with reference to archaeological deposits.* B.Sc. dissertation. London University.
9. BANDI, H. G. et al. (1954) 'Die Brügglihöhle an der Kohlholzholde bei Nenzlingen (Kt. Bern), eine neue Fundstelle des Spätmagdalenien im untern Birstal.' *Jahrb. Bern nat. Hist. Mus.* 32 and 33 (1952–1953): 45–76.
10. BANNISTER, B. (1969) 'Dendrochronology.' In: *Science in Archaeology* (Editors, D. Brothwell and E. Higgs), (2nd edn.), London: 191–205.
11. BARKER, H. (1963) 'The Applications of Radioactivity in Archaeology.' In: *The Scientist and Archaeology* (Editor, E. Pyddoke), London.
12. BARTLETT, H. H. (1956) 'Fire, Primitive Agriculture, and Grazing in the Tropics.' In: *Man's Role in Changing the Face of the Earth* (Editor, W. L. Thomas), Chicago: 692–720.
13. BARTON, L. V. (1961) *Seed Preservation and Longevity.* London.
14. BATTAGLIA, R. (1943) 'La palafitta del Lago di Ledro nel Trentino.' *Memorie Mus. Stor. nat. Venezia trident.* 7: 36.
15. BEADLE, G. W. (1973) 'The origin of *Zea mays*.' In: *The Origins of Agriculture* (Editor, C. A. Reed), The Hague.
16. BERSU, G. (1940) 'Excavations at Little Woodbury, Wiltshire. Part I. The settlement as revealed by excavation.' *Proc. prehist. Soc.* 6: 30–111.
17. BERTSCH, K. (1941) Früchte und Samen. *Handbücher der praktischen Vorgeschichtsforschung.* 1, Stuttgart.

18. BINFORD, L. R. (1972) *An Archaeological Perspective*. New York.
19. BRAIDWOOD, R. J. (1953) 'Did man once live by beer alone?' *Amer. Anthrop.* 55: 515–26.
20. BRUCE-MITFORD, R. (1972) *The Sutton Hoo Ship-Burial*. (2nd edn.), London.
21. BURLEIGH, R. (1974) 'Radiocarbon dating: some practical considerations for the archaeologist.' *J. Archaeol. Sci.* 1: 69–87.
22. CALLEN, E. O. (1969) 'Diet as Revealed by Coprolites.' In: *Science in Archaeology* (Editors, D. Brothwell and E. Higgs), (2nd edn.), London: 235–43.
23. CARPENTER, R. (1946) 'Ancient Rome brought to Life.' *Nat. geogr. Mag.* 90: 567–633.
24. CHATTERS, R. M. (1963) 'Siliceous Skeletons of Wood Fibers.' *Forest Prod. J.* 1963: 368–72.
25. CHILDE, V. G. (1931) *Skara Brae: A Pictish Village in Orkney*. London.
26. CHILDE, V. G. (1965) *Man Makes Himself*. (4th edn.), London.
27. CLARK, J. G. D. (1960). *Star Carr*. Cambridge.
28. CLARK, J. G. D. (1963) 'Neolithic Bows from Somerset, England, and the Prehistory of Archery in North-west Europe.' *Proc. prehist. Soc.* 29: 50–98.
29. CUNNINGTON, M. E. (1929) *Woodhenge*. Devizes.
30. CURWEN, E. C. (1938) 'Early Agriculture in Denmark.' *Antiquity* 12: 135–53.
31. DARBISHIRE, R. D. (1874) 'Notes on Discoveries in Ehenside Tarn, Cumberland.' *Archaeologia* 44: 273–92.
32. DIMBLEBY, G. W. (1952) 'Soil Regeneration on the North-east Yorkshire Moors.' *J. Ecol.* 40: 331–41.
33. DIMBLEBY, G. W. (1955) 'Pollen Analysis as an Aid to the Dating of Prehistoric Monuments.' *Proc. prehist. Soc.* 20: 231–6.
34. DIMBLEBY, G. W. (1961a) 'Transported Material in the Soil Profile.' *J. Soil Sci.* 12: 12–22.
35. DIMBLEBY, G. W. (1961b) 'Soil Pollen Analysis.' *J. Soil Sci.* 12: 1–11.
36. DIMBLEBY, G. W. (1961c) 'The Ancient Forest of Blackamore.' *Antiquity* 35: 123–8.
37. DIMBLEBY, G. W. (1963) 'Pollen Analyses from two Cornish Barrows.' *J. R. Inst. Cornwall* (n.s.) 4: 364–75.
38. DIMBLEBY, G. W. (1976a) 'Landscapes from the past.' *Garten u. Landschaft* 10/76: 591–7.
39. DIMBLEBY, G. W. (1976b) 'Pollen as botanical evidence of the past.' *Landscape Architecture* May, 1976: 219–23.
40. DIMBLEBY, G. W. Unpublished data.
41. DIMBLEBY, G. W., and EVANS, J. G. (1974) 'Pollen and land-snail analysis of calcareous soils.' *J. Archaeol. Sci.* 1: 117–33.
42. DOUGLASS, A. E. (1936) 'The Central Pueblo Chronology.' *Tree-Ring Bull.* 2: 29–34.

43. DUCHAUFOUR, P. (1948) 'Recherches écologiques sur la chênaie atlantique française.' *Annls. Éc. Eaux For.* Nancy 11: 1–332.

44. ELGEE, F. (1930) *Early Man in North-east Yorkshire.* Gloucester.

45. ERDTMAN, G. (1927) 'Peat Deposits of the Cleveland Hills.' *Naturalist, Lond. 1927:* 39–46.

46. ERDTMAN, G. (1952) *Pollen Morphology and Plant Taxonomy. Angiosperms.* Stockholm.

47. ERDTMAN, G., BERGLUND, B., and PRAGLOWSKI, J. (1961) *An Introduction to a Scandinavian Pollen Flora.* Stockholm.

48. EVANS, J. G. and LIMBREY, S. (1974) 'The experimental earthwork on Morden Bog, Wareham, Dorset, England: 1963–72.' *Proc. prehist. Soc.* 40: 170–202.

49. FARRAND, W. R. (1961) 'Frozen mammoths and modern geology.' *Science* 133: 729–35.

50. FARRAR, W. V. (1966) 'Tecuitlatl: A Glimpse of Aztec Food Technology.' *Nature* 211: 341–2.

51. FORBES, R. J. (1958) *Studies in Ancient Technology.* Vol. VI. Leiden.

52. FORSYTH, A. A. (1968) *British Poisonous Plants.* London.

53. GLOB, P. V. (1971) *The Bog People.* London.

54. GODWIN, H. (1960). 'Prehistoric Wooden Trackways of the Somerset Levels: their construction, age and relation to climatic change.' *Proc. prehist. Soc.* 26: 1–36.

55. GODWIN, H. (1968) 'Evidence for longevity of seeds.' *Nature, Lond.* 220: 708–9.

56. GODWIN, H., and CLIFFORD M. H. (1938). 'Studies of the Post-glacial History of British Vegetation. I. Origin and stratigraphy of Fenland deposits near Woodwalton, Hunts. II. Origin and stratigraphy of deposits in Southern Fenland.' *Phil. Trans. R. Soc.* B. 229: 323–406.

57. GODWIN, H., and TALLANTIRE, P. A. (1951) 'Studies of the Post-glacial History of British Vegetation. XII. Hockham Mere, Norfolk.' *New Phytol.* 39: 285–307.

58. GODWIN, H., and TANSLEY, A. G. (1941) 'Prehistoric Charcoals as Evidence of former Vegetation, Soil and Climate.' *J. Ecol.* 29: 117–26.

59. GODWIN, Sir H., and VISHNU-MITTRE (1975) 'Studies of the postglacial history of British Vegetation. XVI Flandrian deposits of the fenland margin at Holme Fen and Whittlesey Mere, Hunts.' *Phil. Trans. R. Soc.* B. 270: 561–608.

60. GODWIN, H., WALKER, D., and WILLIS, E. H. (1957). 'Radiocarbon Dating and Post-glacial Vegetational History: Scaleby Moss.' *Proc. R. Soc.* B. 147: 352–66.

61. GREGORY, P. H. (1961) *The Microbiology of the Atmosphere.* London.

62. HALLAM, J. S. (1960) *The Mesolithic of the Central Pennines.* M.A. Thesis, Liverpool University.

63. HANDLEY, W. R. C. (1954) 'Mull and Mor Formation in Relation to Forest Soils.' *Bull. For. Commn, Lond.* No. 23.

64. HARLAN, J. (1971) 'Agricultural origins: centers and non-centers.' *Science* 174: 468–74.

65. HART, C. E. (1966) *Royal Forest*. Oxford.

66. HAWKES, J. G. (1969) 'The ecological background of plant domestication.' In: *The domestication and exploitation of plants and animals* (Editors, P. J. Ucko and G. W. Dimbleby), London: 17–29.

67. HEIZER, R. F. (1963) 'Domestic Fuel in Primitive Society.' *J. R. anthrop. Inst.*, 93: 186–94.

68. HELBAEK, H. (1953a) 'Early Crops in Southern England.' *Proc. prehist. Soc.* 18: 194–233.

69. HELBAEK, H. (1953b) 'Archaeology and Agricultural Botany.' *Rep. Inst. Archaeol., Lond.* No. 9: 44–59.

70. HELBAEK, H. (1954) 'Prehistoric Food Plants and Weeds in Denmark.' *Danm. geol. Unders.* Series 2, No. 80: 250–61.

71. HELBAEK, H. (1956) 'Vegetables in the Funeral Meals of Pre-urban Rome.' *Acta Instituti romani regni Sueciae*, Series 4, 17: 287–94.

72. HELBAEK, H. (1958) The last meal of Grauballe Man. *Kuml* 1958: 83–116.

73. HELBAEK, H. (1959) Notes on the Evolution and History of *Linum*. *Kuml* 1959: 103–29.

74. HELBAEK, H. (1964) 'First Impressions of the Çatal Hüyük Plant Husbandry.' *Anatolian Studies* 14: 121–3.

75. HELBAEK, H. (1969) 'Palaeo-Ethnobotany.' In: *Science in Archaeology* (Editors, D. Brothwell and E. Higgs), (2nd. edn.) London: 206–14.

76. HILL, J. (1939) *Wild Foods of Britain*. London.

77. HOPF, M. (1969) 'Plant remains and early farming in Jericho.' In: *The domestication and exploitation of plants and animals* (Editors, P. J. Ucko and G. W. Dimbleby), London: 355–9.

78. INGWERSEN, P. (1954) 'Some Microfossils from Danish Late-Tertiary Lignites.' *Danm. geol. Unders.* Series 2, No. 80: 31–64.

79. ISSERLIN, B. S. J. et al. (1964) 'Motya, a Phoenician-Punic Site near Marsala, Sicily.' *Ann. Leeds Univ. Orient. Soc.* 4: 84–131.

80. ITKONEN, T. I. (1938) 'Altertümliche Skier und Schlittenkufen V.' (German summary of Finnish paper). *Suom. Mus.* 45: 33–4.

81. IVERSEN, J. (1941) 'The Influence of Prehistoric Man on Vegetation.' *Danm. geol. Unders.* Series 2, No. 6: 1–25.

82. IVERSEN, J. (1958) 'Pollenanalytischer Nachweis des Reliktencharakters eines jütischen Linden-Mischwaldes.' *Veröff. geobot. Inst., Zürich* 33: 137–44.

83. IVERSEN, J. (1964) 'Retrogressive Vegetational Succession in the Postglacial.' *J. Ecol.* 52. Supplement: 59–70.

84. JACOBI, R. M., TALLIS, J. H., and MELLARS, P. A. (1976) 'The Southern Pennine Mesolithic and the ecological record.' *J. Archaeol. Sci.* 3: 307–20.

85. JARMAN, H. N., LEGGE, A. J., and CHARLES, J. A. (1972) 'Retrieval of plant remains from archaeological sites by froth flotation.' In: *Papers in Economic Prehistory* (Editor, E. S. Higgs), Cambridge.

86. JENNINGS, J. D. and NORBECK, E. (Editors) (1964) *Prehistoric Man in the New World*. Chicago.

87. JEWELL, P. A. (Editor) (1963) *The Experimental earthwork on Overton Down, Wiltshire, 1960*. London.

88. JEWELL, P. A., and DIMBLEBY, G. W. (1966) 'The Experimental Earthwork on Overton Down: The first four years.' *Proc. prehist. Soc.* **32**: 313–42.

89. JOHNSON, F., and RAUP, H. M. (1964) 'Investigations in South-west Yukon: Geobotanical and Archaeological Reconnaissance.' *Pap. Robert S. Peabody Fdn. Archaeol.* **6**: 1–198.

90. JONASSEN, H. (1950) 'Recent Pollen Sedimentation and Jutland Heath Diagrams.' *Dansk bot. Ark.* **13**: 1–168.

91. JONES, E. W. (1944) 'Biological flora of the British Isles. *Acer pseudoplatanus* L.' *J. Ecol.* **32**: 220–37.

92. JONGERIUS, A. (1956) 'Étude micromorphologique des sols sableux secs des bois et bruyères au Pays-Bas.' *Trans. 6th. int. Congr. Soil Sci.*, Paris, E: 353–7.

93. KEEF, P. A. M., WYMER, J. J., and DIMBLEBY, G. W. (1965) 'A Mesolithic Site on Iping Common, Sussex, England.' *Proc. prehist. Soc.* **31**: 85–92.

94. KEEPAX, C. (1975) 'Scanning electron microscopy of wood replaced by iron corrosion products.' *J. Archaeol. Sci.* **2**: 145–50.

95. KEILLER, A. (1965) *Windmill Hill and Avebury*. Oxford.

96. KIRBY, R. H. (1963) *Vegetable Fibres*. London.

97. KOSTREWSKI, J. (1938) 'Biskupin: an early Iron Age village in Western Poland.' *Antiquity* **12**: 311–17.

98. LAURING, P. (1957). *Land of the Tollund Man*. London.

99. LEE, R. B., and DE VORE, I. (Editors) (1965) *Man the Hunter*. Chicago.

100. LENEY, L., and CASTEEL, R. W. (1975) 'Simplified procedure for examining charcoal specimens for identification.' *J. Archaeol. Sci.* **2**: 153–9.

101. LUTZ, H. J. (1959) 'Aboriginal Man and White Man as Historical Causes of Fires in the Boreal Forest, with particular reference to Alaska.' *Yale Univ. Sch. For. Bull.* No. 65.

102. MABEY, R. (1972) *Food for Free*. London.

103. MACKERETH, F. J. H. (1965) 'Chemical Investigations of Lake Sediments and their Interpretation.' In: 'A Discussion on the Development of Habitats in the post-Glacial.' *Proc. R. Soc. B.* **161**: 283–309.

104. MCVEAN, D. N. (1956) 'Ecology of *Alnus glutinosa* (L) Gaertn. VI. Postglacial history.' *J. Ecol.* **44**: 331–3.

105. MANGELSDORF, P. (1974) *Corn*. Cambridge, Mass.

106. MANGELSDORF, P. C., MACNEISH, R. S., and WILEY, G. R. (1971) 'Origins of agriculture in middle America.' In: *Prehistoric Agriculture* (Editor, S. Struever), New York.

107. MARTIN, P. S. (1963) *The Last 10,000 Years*. Tucson.

108. MARTIN, P. S., SABELS, B. E., and SHUTLER, D. (1961) 'Rampart Cave Coprolite and Ecology of the Shasta Ground Sloth.' *Am. J. Sci.* **295**: 102–27.

109. MATTHEWS, J. D. (1955) 'The Influence of Weather on the Frequency of Beech Mast Years in England.' *Forestry* **28**: 107–16.
110. METCALFE, C. R. (1960) *Anatomy of the Monocotyledons. I. Gramineae.* Oxford.
111. MONEY, J. H. (1960) 'Excavations at High Rocks, Tunbridge Wells, 1954–1956.' *Sussex archaeol. Collections.* **98**: 173–221.
112. MOORE, P. D. (1973) 'The influence of prehistoric cultures upon the initiation and spread of blanket bog in upland Wales.' *Nature, Lond.* **241**: 350–3.
113. MOORE, P. D. (1974) 'Prehistoric human activity and blanket peat initiation on Exmoor.' *Nature, Lond.* **250**: 439–41.
114. MOWAT, F. (1952) *People of the Deer.* London.
115. NEUSTUPNY, J. (1952) 'Alliaceous plants in prehistory and history.' *Archiv Orientálné.* **20**: 356–85.
116. NORDHAGEN, R. (1954) 'Om barkebrød og treslaget alm i Kulturhistorisk belysning.' *Danm. geol. Unders.* Series 2, No. 80: 262–308.
117. NORTH, P. M. (1967) *Poisonous Plants and Fungi.* London.
118. NÚÑEZ, M. G., and VUORELA, I. (1976) 'A field method for the retrieval of plant remains from archaeological sites.' *Memoranda Soc. Fauna Flora Fennica* **52**: 19–22.
119. PEARSALL, W. H. (1965) (Organizer). 'A Discussion on the Development of Habitats in the post-Glacial.' *Proc. R. Soc.* B. **161**: 293–375.
120. PEARSALL, W. H., and PENNINGTON, W. (1973) *The Lake District.* London.
121. PENNINGTON, W. (1965) 'The Interpretation of some post-Glacial Vegetation Diversities at different Lake District Sites.' In: 'A Discussion on the Development of Habitats in the post-Glacial.' *Proc. R. Soc.* B. **161**: 310–23.
122. PETERSON, R. F. (1965) *Wheat.* London.
123. PHILLIPS, E. D. (1965) *The Royal Hordes – Nomad Peoples of the Steppes.* London.
124. PICKERSGILL, B. (1969) 'The domestication of chili peppers.' In: *The domestication and exploitation of plants and animals* (Editors, P. J. Ucko and G. W. Dimbleby), London: 443–50.
125. PIGGOTT, S. (1954) *The Neolithic Cultures of the British Isles.* Cambridge.
126. PIKE, G. (1965) 'Recent Evidence for Land Transport in Europe outside the Mediterranean Area before the Late Bronze Age.' *Bull. Inst. Archaeol., Lond.* **5**: 45–60.
127. PITTIONI, R. (1951) 'Prehistoric Copper-Mining in Austria: Problems and Facts.' *Rep. Inst. Archaeol., Lond.* No. 7: 16–43.
128. POSENER, G. (1962) *A Dictionary of Egyptian Civilization.* London.
129. PROUDFOOT, V. B. (1958) 'Problems of Soil History. Podzol Development at Goodland and Torr Townlands, Co. Antrim, N. Ireland.' *J. Soil Sci.* **9**: 186–98.
130. RABIEN, I. (1953) 'Zur Bestimmung fossiler Knospenschupfen.' *Paläont. Z.* **27**: 57–66.
131. RAMSBOTTOM, J. (1953) *Mushrooms and Toadstools.* London.

132. RANKINE, W. F., RANKINE, W. M., and DIMBLEBY, G. W. (1960) 'Further Excavations at a Mesolithic Site at Oakhanger, Selborne, Hants.' *Proc. prehist. Soc.* **26**: 246–62.

133. RENFREW, J. M., MONK, M., and MURPHY, P. (n.d.) *First aid for seeds.* Hertford.

134. RILEY, R. (1969) 'Evidence from phylogenetic relationships of the types of bread wheat first cultivated.' In: *The domestication and exploitation of plants and animals* (Editors, P. J. Ucko and G. W. Dimbleby), London: 173–6.

135. ROUX, I., and LEROI-GOURHAN, Arl. (1965) 'Les défrichements de la période atlantique.' *Bull. Soc. préhist. fr.* *(1964)* **61**: 309–15.

136. SALISBURY, E. J., and JANE, F. W. (1940) 'Charcoals from Maiden Castle and their Significance in relation to the Vegetation and Climatic Conditions in Prehistoric Times.' *J. Ecol.* **28**: 310–25.

137. SAUER, C. O. (1963) 'Fire and Early Man.' In: *Land and Life*, Berkeley, California: 288–99.

138. SCHERMAN, K. (1976) *Iceland: Daughter of Fire.* London.

139. SCHÜTRUMPF, R. (1958) 'Die pollenanalytische Untersuchung der neuen Moorleichen aus dem Kreis Eckernförde.' *Prähist. Z.* **36**: 156–66.

140. SCUDDER, T. (1962) *The Ecology of the Gwembe Tonga.* Manchester.

141. SEAGRIEF, S. C. (1959) 'Pollen Diagrams from Southern England: Wareham, Dorset, and Nursling, Hampshire. *New Phytol.* **58**: 316–25.

142. SEAWARD, M. R. D., CROSS, T., and UNSWORTH, B. A. (1976) 'Viable bacterial spores recovered from an archaeological excavation.' *Nature, Lond.* **261**: 407–8.

143. SEAWARD, M. R. D., and WILLIAMS, D. (1976) 'The interpretation of mosses found in recent archaeological investigations.' *J. Archaeol. Sci.* **3**: 173–7.

144. SIMMONS, I. G. (1964) 'Pollen Diagrams from Dartmoor.' *New Phytol.* **63**: 165–80.

145. SIMMONS, I. G. (1975) 'The ecological setting of mesolithic man in the Highland Zone.' In: *The Effect of Man on the Environment: The Highland Zone* (Editors, J. G. Evans, S. Limbrey, and H. Cleere), London: 57–63.

146. SIMMONS, I. G., ATHERDEN, M. A., CUNDILL, P. R., and JONES, R. L. (1975) 'Inorganic layers in soligenous mires of the North Yorkshire Moors.' *J. Biogeogr.* **2**: 49–56.

147. SIMMONS, I. G., and DIMBLEBY, G. W. (1974) 'The possible role of ivy (*Hedera helix* L.) in the mesolithic economy of Western Europe.' *J. Archaeol. Sci.* **1**: 291–6.

148. SMARTT, J. (1969) 'Evolution of American *Phaseolus* beans under domestication.' In: *The domestication and exploitation of plants and animals* (Editors, P. J. Ucko and G. W. Dimbleby), London: 451–62.

149. SMITH, A. G. (1970) 'The influence of mesolithic and neolithic man on British vegetation.' In: *Studies in the vegetation history of the British Isles* (Editors, D. Walker and R. G. West.), Cambridge: 81–96.

150. SMITH, M. A. (1957) 'The Shuttlestone Barrow, Parwich (Derbyshire).' *Inventaria Archaeologica* 4th set. G.B. 19.

151. SMITHSON, F. (1958) 'Grass Opal in British soils.' *J. Soil Sci.* **9**: 148–54.

152. SOLECKI, R. S. (1963) 'Prehistory in Shanidar Valley, Northern Iraq.' *Science*, N.Y. **139**: 179–93.

153. STEENSBERG, A. (1976) 'The husbandry of food production.' *Phil. Trans. R. Soc.* B. **275**: 43–54.

154. STEWART, O. C. (1956) 'Fire as the First Great Force Employed by Man.' In: *Man's Role in Changing the Face of the Earth* (Editor, W. L. Thomas), Chicago.

155. STRUEVER, S. (1971) *Prehistoric Agriculture.* New York.

156. SUESS, H. E. (1970) 'Bristlecone pine calibration of the radiocarbon time-scale 5200 BC to the present.' In: *Radiocarbon Variations and Absolute Chronology* (Editor, I. U. Olsson), Chichester: 303–11.

157. SWART, E. R. (1963) 'Age of the Baobab tree.' *Nature, Lond.* **198**: 708–9.

158. THOMPSON, M. W., ASHBEE, P., and DIMBLEBY, G. W. (1957) 'Excavation of a Barrow near the Hardy Monument, Black Down, Portesham, Dorset.' *Proc. prehist. Soc.* **23**: 124–36.

159. THURSTAN, V. (1965) *The Use of Vegetable Dyes.* (9th edn.), Leicester.

160. TROELS-SMITH, J. (1956) 'Neolithic Period in Switzerland and Denmark.' *Science*, N.Y. **124**: 876–9.

161. TROELS-SMITH, J. (1959) 'An elmetraes-bue fra Aamosen.' *Aarborger fr. Nordisk oldkind. hist. 1959*: 91–145.

162. TROELS-SMITH, J. (1960a) 'The Muldbjerg Dwelling Place: An Early Neolithic archaeological Site in the Aamosen Bog, West Zealand, Denmark.' *Smiths. Rep. for 1959*: 577–601.

163. TROELS-SMITH, J. (1960b) 'Ivy, Mistletoe and Elm. Climate Indicators – Fodder Plants.' *Danm. geol. Unders.* Series 4, **4**: 4–32.

164. TUBBS, C. R., and DIMBLEBY, G. W. (1965) 'Early Agriculture in the New Forest.' *Advnct. Sci. Lond.* **22**: 88–97.

165. TURNER, J. (1962) 'The *Tilia* decline: an anthropogenic interpretation.' *New Phytol.* **61**: 328–41.

166. TURNER, J. (1965) 'A Contribution to the History of Forest Clearance.' In: 'A Discussion on the Development of Habitat in the post-Glacial.' *Proc. R. Soc.* B. **161**: 343–53.

167. VOGT, E. (1949) 'Birch as a Source of Raw Material during the Stone Age.' *Proc. prehist. Soc.* **15**: 50–1.

168. WAALS, J. D. van der (1964) *Prehistoric Disc Wheels in the Netherlands.* Groningen.

169. WALLWORK, J. A. (1970) *Ecology of Soil Animals.* London.

170. WATERBOLK, H. T. (1954) *De praehistorische mens en zijn milieu.* Rijksuniversiteit te Groningen.

171. WATLING, R., and SEAWARD, M. R. D. (1976) 'Some observations on puff-balls from British archaeological sites.' *J. Archaeol. Sci.* **3**: 165–72.

172. WELLS, C. (1964) *Bones, Bodies and Disease.* London.

173. WEST, R. G. (1956) 'The Quaternary Deposits at Hoxne, Suffolk.' *Phil. Trans. R. Soc.* B. **239**: 265–356.

174. WESTERN, A. C. (1969) 'Wood and Charcoal in Archaeology.' In: *Science in Archaeology* (Editors, D. Brothwell and E. Higgs), (2nd edn.), London: 178–87.

175. WHITAKER, T. W., CUTLER, H. C., and MACNEISH, R. S. (1957) 'Cucurbit materials from three caves near Ocampo, Tamaulipas.' *Amer. Antiq.* **22**: 352–8.

176. WHYTE, R. O. (1973) 'An environmental interpretation of the origin of Asian cereals.' *Indian J. Genetics Plant Breeding.* 34A: 1–11.

177. WHYTE, R. O. (in press) 'An environmental interpretation of the origin of Asian food legumes.' *Indian J. Genetics Plant Breeding.*

178. WILLIAMS, D. (1976a) 'A neolithic moss flora from Silbury Hill, Wiltshire.' *J. Archaeol. Sci.* **3**: 267–70.

179. WILLIAMS, D. (1976b) 'Bryophytes in Archaeology.' *Science and Archaeology* No. 18: 12–14.

180. WILLIS, E. H. (1969) 'Radiocarbon Dating.' In: *Science in Archaeology* (Editors, D. Brothwell and E. Higgs), (2nd edn.), London: 46–57.

181. WRIGHT, E. V., and CHURCHILL, D. M. (1965) 'The Boats from North Ferriby, Yorkshire, England, with a review of the origins of the sewn boats of the Bronze Age.' *Proc. prehist. Soc.* **31**: 1–24.

182. WRIGHT, H. E. (1976) 'The environmental setting for plant domestication in the Near East.' *Science* **194**: 385–9.

183. WYMER, J. (1959) 'Excavations on the Mesolithic Site at Thatcham, Berks., 1958.' *Berks. archaeol. J.* **57**: 1–33.

184. van ZEIST, W. (1974) 'Palaeobotanical studies of settlement sites in the coastal area of the Netherlands.' *Palaeohistoria* **16**: 223–371.

185. van ZEIST, W., and BAKKER-HEERES, J. A. H. (1975) 'Evidence for linseed cultivation before 6000 bc' *J. Archaeol. Sci.* **2**: 215–19.

186. ZEUNER, F. E. (1958) *Dating the Past.* (4th edn.), London.

187. ZOHARY, D. (1969) 'The progenitors of wheat and barley in relation to domestication and agricultural dispersal in the Old World.' In: *The domestication and exploitation of plants and animals* (Editors, P. J. Ucko and G. W. Dimbleby), London: 47–66.

Index

Index

syrup, 28, 36
Marigold, marsh, 31
Martin, P. S., 116
Mast years, 35
Meadowsweet, 52
Mediterranean, 34, 75, 77, 84
Medlar, 32
Mercurialis perennis, 52
Mesolithic, 26, 32, 34, 35, 37, 54, 59, 118, 128, 139, 140, 142, 149, 150, 152, 161
Mesopotamia, 77
Mespilus, 32
Mexico, 80, 81, 82
  City, 38
Millets, 33
Mimosa, 49
Mining, 64–5
Mistletoe, 140
Moldenke, H. N. and A. L., 38
Moonwort, 122
Moore, P. D., 150
Moorland, 142, 143, 144, 151
Moravia, 70
Moringa, 69
Moss, hair, 47, 51, 60
Mosses, 54, 60, 122, 133
Motya, Sicily, 62
Mountain avens, 23
Mucilage, 50, 132
Mud-brick, 42, 43, 98
Mugwort, 141
Mullein, 130
Multiple perforation plates, 100, 109
Mummification, 68–9
Mummy wheat, 129
Musical instruments, 55
Myrobalanus, 49
Myrrh, 68

Near East, 49, 73, 74, 75, 76, 81, 128, 129, 139
Neckera complanata, 60
Nectar, 32
Needles, 47

Nelumbo lutea, 37
Neolithic, 37, 45, 46, 49, 54, 62, 66, 70, 71, 77, 79, 118, 121, 140, 143, 144, 153, 154, 161, 162
Nets, 63
Nettle, stinging, 31, 47, 85, 112
Neustupny, J., 70
New Forest, 59, 142
Nightshade, black, 127
  deadly, 40
Nile Valley, 145
Noin Ula, Russia, 93
Nuphar, 28, 32
Nymphaea, 28, 32
Nyssa sylvatica, 62

Oak, 34, 35, 42, 44, 49, 53, 57, 58, 59, 61, 63, 64, 69, 94, 96, 97, 103, 104, 105, 109, 141, 143, 145, 150, 153, 154, 160, 161
  sessile, 59
  white, 35
Oakhanger, Hants, 140
Oats, 33, 79, 128
Ocampo, Mexico, 81, 82
Offa's Dyke, 64
Oil, 27, 54, 70
  almond, 69
  balanos, 69
  ben, 69
  castor, 55, 69
  cedar, 69
  ducts, 101
  hempseed, 50
  linseed, 50, 54, 84
  olive, 55
Onion, 28, 51
Ophioglossum vulgatum, 122
Orchids, 126
Orkneys, 45
Osmunda regalis, 122

Pacific Islands, 48
Palaeolithic, 49, 54, 61, 138, 139, 150, 161
Palms, 46, 84

ARCHAEOLOGY

BEFORE THE DELUGE   Herbert Wendt   90p
Palaeontology sets out to find the point in the past when life began
to exist on our planet, how it developed, and when man first
appeared. This is the story of how palaeontology developed as a
science and what it now tells us about the planet on which we live.
Illustrated.

MYSTERIOUS BRITAIN   Janet and Colin Bord   £1.95
All over the British countryside are totems and indications of lost
civilisations and knowledge, scattered in a rich profusion if only the
eye can see. This book looks into the past while suggesting some
startling research for the future. Illustrated.

THE SECRET COUNTRY   Janet and Colin Bord   £1.95
More Mysterious Britain. An exploration of folklore,
legends and hauntings surrounding the standing stones,
earthworks and ancient carvings of Britain.

THE CHANGING FACE OF BRITAIN   Edward Hyams   £1.50
Illustrated general study of how the geological structure of the land,
our climate, our social history and our industries have contributed
to the shape of our landscape.

THE DAWN OF EUROPEAN CIVILISATION
V. Gordon Childe   £1.00
The last edition of the classic archaeological work that continues to
dominate all explanations of the growth of European prehistory.
Illustrated.

*All these books are available at your local bookshop or newsagent, or can
be ordered direct from the publisher. Just tick the titles you want and fill
in the form below.*

Name ....

Address ....

....

Write to Paladin Cash Sales, PO Box 11, Falmouth, Cornwall
TR10 9EN.
Please enclose remittance to the value of the cover price plus:
UK: 22p for the first book plus 10p per copy for each additional book
ordered to a maximum charge of 82p.
BFPO and EIRE: 22p for the first book plus 10p per copy for the next
6 books, thereafter 3p per book.
OVERSEAS: 30p for the first book and 10p for each additional book.
*Granada Publishing reserve the right to show new retail prices on covers,
which may differ from those previously advertised in the text or elsewhere.*